The Process of Dramaturgy

A Handbook

The Process of Dramaturgy

A Handbook

Scott R. Irelan
Augustana College (IL)

Anne Fletcher
Southern Illinois University Carbondale

Julie Felise Dubiner
Actors Theatre of Louisville

Table of Contents

Acknowledgments and Thanks

Scott

To all dramaturgy students at Illinois State University and Augustana College—in particular Leah Hansen, Heidi Nees, Jeff LaRocque, Brian Bengston, Katie Wyant, Katie McCarthy, Heather Tealbey, Liz Riordan, Gabi Schaffranick, Jen Altenbernd, Rachel Stearns, Krista Johnson, Danielle Swanson, Amy Sanders, Matthew Fox, David Cocks, and Veronica Smith. To directors James Russell Couch, Ron Clark, Kristin Horton, Catherine Weidner, Bill Jenkins, Deb Alley, Jeff Coussens, Donna Hare-McNider, Mark Hurty and so many others for fostering such wonderful creative-collaborative environments in which to work. To faculty and staff collaborators Adam Parboosingh, Ellen Dixon, Andy Gutshall, Anna Hurty, John Poole, and Ann Haugo. To all the writers who have given me the honor of developing their work, especially Jon Ray Sheline, Jon Myers and Dana Formby. To my family for encouraging my dramaturgical work though they are not always clear as to what it is exactly.

Anne

To all dramaturgy students at Winthrop University—Fulton Burns, Jenna Derrick Cartee, Mary Cipolla French, Bryan Gant, Nicia Feldman Moore, Chris O'Neill—and at Southern Illinois University Carbondale, in particular Steve Ackerman, Jennifer Caudell, Randall Colburn, Ellen Conn, Ken Ellis, Amy France, Jessica Johnson Frohling, Michael Frohling, Nick Jones, Kiri Tussing-Palm, Emily Kelly-Padden, Margie Pignataro, Neal Ryan Shaw, Patricia Pfeiffer Sherman, Shelley Stubbs, and Jordan Vakselis. To directors Segun Ojewuyi, Jenny Holcombe, Tom Kidd, Lori Merrill-Fink as well as to faculty collaborators Bob Holcombe, Ron Naversen, Kathryn Wagner, and Sarah J. Blackstone, and so many others that I am unable to list them here.

Julie

To Actors Theatre of Louisville's artistic department, especially the dramaturgy/literary staff and interns; and always thanks to the writers, directors, designers, casts, crews, and staff who make the main stage season and Humana Festival so fabulous. A special thank you to Matthew Callahan, Liz Engelman, LMDA, Defiant Theatre, blue star performance company, Steppenwolf and all theaters who have supported the work of freelance dramaturgs.

Special acknowledgment and thanks to:
- Ron Pullins and all the folks at Focus Publishing for believing in this project
- Augustana College's Office of the Dean for financial support through the New Faculty Research Fund
- Jonathan Myers for his uncanny ability to make connections

Introduction

Committing Acts of Dramaturgy

The Process of Dramaturgy: A Handbook reflects upon the lively, imaginative practice of production dramaturgy from an experiential perspective. It offers a series of workable strategies and practical exercises meant not only to develop and improve but also to expand and extend sensibilities and skill sets often used when communicating with directors, designers, playwrights, front of house staff, education and outreach teams, and spectators. *The Process of Dramaturgy* argues that someone need not be either a scholar or historian to recognize the web(s) of connection(s) innate to producing a live theatrical performance event. In the end, our primary goal is to offer ways in to committing "acts of dramaturgy" regardless of whether someone is a classroom learner, one-person drama department, regional theatre intern, or early career professional intrigued by approaches to the craft as they learn on the job. This book is also meant for those who self-identify as director, designer, performer, and the like in that it discusses avenues of engagement for productive creative-collaboration with a production dramaturg. We hope to open a dialogue among practitioners regarding the integration of not only dramaturgical processes but also a production dramaturg into their overall preparation.

How This Book Came to Be

The Process of Dramaturgy emerges from the presupposition that dramaturgical acts are committed wherever individuals come together in an environment of support for creative relationships explicitly in the name of crafting a **live performance event**. Striving to achieve a **unified production**, the **production team**—traditionally guided by the director—reaches consensus regarding **thematic concerns**, **concept**, and **style of production**. Often production goals include making connections within a larger social and cultural context; reaching out to a broader community; expanding the live performance event to create an extended dialogue in the forms of pre-show programming, theatre tours and even symposia. In settings where filling all of the positions on the ideal organizational chart is improbable if not impossible, the tasks of creating these para-theatrical (and often interdisciplinary) experiences fall to directors, classroom instructors, interns and apprentices, designers, or a cadre of interested volunteers. Even in larger, more affluent professional companies or conservatory training programs, the tasks we think of as belonging to the production dramaturg manifest themselves in the offices of literary managers, educational outreach coordinators, or even public information officers and marketing specialists. This being the case, we work to create a discursive space of investigation through both active learning exercises and case study.

Since no strict model of "production dramaturgy" has necessarily emerged in either theory or practice, our stated task is immediately complicated. Definitions of the word itself are contested and the employment of a theatre practitioner, a "production dramaturg", has come to connote countless and wide-ranging undertakings and responsibilities—none of which are ever really defined in the same ways from venue to venue. In explaining what we do as production dramaturgs, we often explain ourselves as the person(s) who conduct(s) pre-production research that contributes to the overall look and feel of the show. During the rehearsal and production phases, we think of the production dramaturg as "story manager" or "continuity specialist" who works with creative-collaborators to ensure the story being told is uniform visually, aurally and in outreach materials as well as in the live performance event itself. In any event, the production dramaturg's tasks have been employed in the crafting of dramatic productions since the early days of Western theatre. Though the named role of "production dramaturg" is still relatively new to Western theatre (as is "the director"), someone has always done the tasks now equated with those of the production dramaturg—critiquing the script, completing historical/background research, monitoring unity in rehearsals and production meetings, etcetera. It is safe to presume that as playwright, actor and choreographer Aeschylus almost certainly served as his own production dramaturg. Years later, the European roots of production dramaturgy were codified and more clearly defined by the works of **Denis Diderot** and **Gotthold Ephraim Lessing**. While essentially critics, it is from their experiences and essays that many get the idea that the production dramaturg is an erudite theorist or stern scholar—roles often foreign to the daily life of those not self-identifying as academics or professional production dramaturgs. *The Process of Dramaturgy*, however, does not necessarily concern itself with the storied history and definition of production dramaturgy, the historicized role of the production dramaturg, script analysis techniques, or even methods of playwriting per se. It does, however, concern itself with processes inherent in completing tasks that usually fall under the purview of a designated production dramaturg. In short, this book emerges from our belief that many of the responsibilities inherent to the Diderot-Lessing legacy revert to *someone* and it is to that *someone* we address *The Process of Dramaturgy*.

For our purposes here we think of this legacy not as a laundry list of "must haves" but rather as buffet menu from which to choose when considering which tasks might come together the best in order to facilitate storytelling as a play text makes its way from the page to the stage. These include but are certainly not limited to:

- sorting out elements of genre and style or diagramming structure as a way to seek out patterns and rhythms, or listing the given circumstances of each scene and seeking out images and other resources as points of inspiration and clarification.
- surveying the language for clues to intrinsic meaning(s), innuendo, double-entendre and the like
- identifying fantastical moments in need of special attention (i.e. blood work, funeral ritual, drag show)
- asking a writer where they were when they wrote the newest play or reading hundreds of plays to find fresh perspectives
- sitting in previews taking notes, not only as a pair of "critical eyes" but also as a spectator responding to a live performance
- sharing with spectators insights that will enrich their engagement in the live performance event.

The most important choices, however, are always those that provide ways to find a personal connection with the play, or at least ways in which the written text intersects with daily lived experiences. Ultimately, the notion of committing "acts of dramaturgy" appeals to us as practitioners because rather than setting hard, definitional parameters—which are counter to the spirit of collaboration—it allows us to recognize that dramaturgy is a highly individualized process with a multiplicity of tasks that are, at times, difficult to codify as truisms for all productions. This point of view also allows us to argue that it is the production dramaturg—the "continuity specialist"—who emerges as the creative-collaborator most frequently moving from the quiet corners of the library into the dynamic rehearsal space and back again in order to engage collaborators, to test artistic choices so as to clarify them, to advocate for both the written text and the spectator who will soon arrive to see that text in performance, and so much more, in the name of enriched, unified storytelling. Turning to theatre history for an analogy, we might consider the contemporary production dramaturg as somewhat akin to the Greek Chorus—furthering the action, flashing back to the past, probing, questioning, and (when solicited) offering advice. Lastly, though the production examples we provide are drawn from our work with US theatres of varying size and scope, the issues and themes we address are broadly applicable to production dramaturgy as a process regardless of theatrical venue or geographical boundary.

What This Book Is and Is Not

Several of the books currently available for study focus almost entirely on the definition of "the production dramaturg", the history of production dramaturgy, the production dramaturg's functions in literary offices, and the struggles to be validated within the live theatrical production process. They are typically collections of essays by practicing production dramaturgs or literary managers, transcripts of interviews between directors and production dramaturgs, or process articles specific to a single production. Examples include, but are not limited to, *Dramaturgy in the American Theatre* edited by Susan Jonas, Geoff Proehl and Michael Lupu; *Between the Lines* edited by

Judith Rudakoff and Lynn Thomson, and *What is Dramaturgy?* edited by Bert Cardullo. While quite informative and useful in their own right, the target audience for these particular compilations seems to be established professionals and seasoned academics. In contrast, our intention is to broaden the scope of inquiry to meet the needs of production dramaturgs whatever their education level or professional standing. Additionally, *What is Dramaturgy* (though in its third reprinting) is fourteen years old, *Between the Lines* is over five years old, and *Dramaturgy in the American Theatre* is more than ten years old. In the time since these editions were first released there has been a consistent critical reappraisal of production dramaturgy and the role of the production dramaturg (and literary manager for that matter). This trend is best exemplified by *Dramaturgy and Performance* by Cathy Turner and Synne Behrndt in which the authors review a variety of perspectives on the term "production dramaturgy". Other recent examples include *Dramaturgy: A Revolution in Theatre* in which Mary Luckhurst covers the history of the origins of production dramaturgs, literary managers and play doctors, as well as Andrew Hartley's *The Shakespearean Dramaturg: A Theoretical and Practical Guide*. While offering some practical tips in handbook format much like *The Process of Dramaturgy*, Hartley's work, as the title indicates, is limited by its period-specific content and scope. Additionally, Geoffrey S. Proehl's *Toward a Dramaturgical Sensibility: Landscape and Journey* wrestles with similar issues, though the author's highly reflective tone distinguishes it from the others. While there is little by way of explicit "how to" for the neophyte production dramaturg, Proehl's work does further the discussion about dramaturgy, the production dramaturg and the necessity of each in theatre and live performance in a unique and worthwhile way. Because the field of production dramaturgy is so expansive both in practice and in definition, a broad range of texts are necessary for coursework regarding production dramaturgy, its history and the role(s) of the production dramaturg. We recommend any combination of the abovementioned texts as supplements to *The Process of Dramaturgy*.[1]

The Process of Dramaturgy fills a gap, then, by specifically calling particular attention to the myriad ways in which an individual might go about developing a production dramaturg's aesthetic sensibility on the road to committing "acts of dramaturgy" in the production process. Given the seeming dearth of practical guides to production dramaturgy and taking into account the precipitous rise in the number of course offerings at both colleges and universities, our discussion explores ways of initiating conversations about "named" or "unnamed" dramaturgical acts, which are an integral part of a production and worthy of further exploration. What makes *The Process of Dramaturgy* truly unique is the way in which it suggests a place of symbiosis between research and creative interpretation that clearly connects analysis to the live performance event.

Admittedly no one handbook can fully explicate, demonstrate, or even elucidate the multiplicity of perspectives, lenses and approaches to the production dramaturgy process. In fact, following any practical guide, no matter how well crafted, to the letter is no way to become a well-rounded practitioner. It is through mentorship, on the job training and a lifelong pursuit of learning that someone becomes an effective, trusted dramaturg. *The Process of Dramaturgy* offers a way to begin this journey. Accordingly, notions of "active", "creative" and "practical" continually guide our thinking and discussion as we move through a series of best practices drawn from our collective work as academic and professional production dramaturgs. Furthermore, the exercises provided within each chapter have been tested and refined by both graduate and undergraduate students as well as interns and apprentices. Moreover, the techniques, paradigms, and methodologies offered here have, time and again, proven quite useful in our own production work, having been vetted in professional venues such as the Actors Theatre of Louisville, Boston Playwrights' Theatre, Riverside Theatre Shakespeare Festival, the St. Louis Black Repertory Theatre, and others. In the

---

1   For those specifically interested in theoretical underpinnings of UK and European dramaturgy, we recommend consulting both *Dramaturgy: A Revolution in Theatre* and *Dramaturgy and Performance*. For a broad Canadian perspective, we suggest the first portion of *Between the Lines*.

end, we not only point to personal qualities and insights from which a dramaturgical sensibility might emerge but also offer a basic set of proficiencies that will enhance any production process.

How This Book is Organized

Structurally we divide *The Process of Dramaturgy* into three distinct parts—**Pre-Production**, Rehearsal, and In Production—so as to emulate the major phases common to the production process of directors, designers, education/outreach departments and the like. Part One is composed of three chapters. *Chapter One: Laying the Groundwork* outlines some conventional hunting and gathering tasks frequently done prior to a first meeting with the director. Using the research work from the first chapter, *Chapter Two: Opening a Dialogue* discusses a shift from compiling information to opening a dialogue with the director. *Chapter Three: Conceptual Frameworks* is dedicated to recognizing patterns across time/history, engaging significant ideas in somewhat insignificant tasks and engendering conversation so as to avoid stasis.

We begin Part Two with *Chapter Four: An Eye for Continuity*. Broad in scope yet focused in purpose, this chapter looks at tasks such as preparing and editing a classic text, the development of production resource packets, developing outreach ideas, and the like. Shifting gears slightly *Chapter Five: The New Play* discusses challenges faced by the dramaturg when working with a living playwright on a yet-to-be-produced play. This chapter focuses on developing a safe and trust-filled relationship between the writer, production dramaturg and production team.

Part Three encompasses *Chapter Six: Outreach and Education*, which looks at how to expand the live theatrical performance event into a larger dialogue, and *Chapter Seven: A Case Study of* Biloxi Blues that integrates and synthesizes the techniques and tactics we talk about across the entire book. *Chapter Eight* offers some closing thoughts for student dramaturgs and instructors. Though *The Process of Dramaturgy* is partitioned this way for organizational purposes, it is vital to remember that many tasks and processes inherent to committing acts of dramaturgy overlap in ways that cannot be illustrated fully in print.

Lastly, we use a variety of texts as primary examples, all of which are readily available in print. They are:

Biloxi Blues, Neil Simon

Dancing at Lughnasa, Brian Friel

My Fair Lady, Alan Jay Lerner with music by Frederick Loewe

On the Verge, Eric Overmyer

Our Town, Thornton Wilder

The Complete Works of William Shakespeare (abridged),
     Borgeson, Long and Singer

The Taming of the Shrew, William Shakespeare

Titus Andronicus, William Shakespeare

We also make references to:

A Christmas Carol, Charles Dickens (adaptations by Couch &
     Irelan as well as Field)

A Raisin in the Sun, Lorraine Hansberry

Death and the King's Horseman, Wole Soyinka

Nickel and Dimed, Joan Holden

Richard III, William Shakespeare

The Crucible, Arthur Miller

The Tempest, William Shakespeare

The Underpants, adapted by Steve Martin from *Die Hose*

The full bibliographic information for these chosen example texts is located in Appendix C.

An Exercise on Beginning: Taking Stock

Anyone who has already investigated some of the available literature on production dramaturgy may be intimidated by sources claiming a fluency in several languages (or at least reading knowledge) as a prerequisite or emphasizing that a firm grasp of literary theory is fundamental. While these skills can only enhance the productivity of a production dramaturg, they can be acquired as practitioners continue to learn and grow. Nevertheless, everyone already possesses untold abilities, gifts and aptitudes that will contribute greatly to work as a production dramaturg regardless of education.

We have employed this exercise in production dramaturgy classrooms, and learners have reflected on it as confidence-building and practical. It can be experienced in a class or with a group, or can be completed in private, reflecting on the resultant data.

Instructions

1. Make a list of all the courses or training you remember from your past that might be applied to production dramaturgy, or simply might relate to any play script you can imagine. ***You MAY NOT include theatre-related training or coursework.***

2. Now make a "wish list" of (non-theatre) areas you would like to explore—in a classroom or in a less formal classroom setting.

Sample List of Courses or Training

- Life-guarding
- Science for Non-Science Majors
- Art History
- Piano Lessons
- Sociology
- Geography
- American History
- Creative Crafts
- World Religions
- Played in an orchestra
- Played Field Hockey and Basketball
- Modern Dance
- Attended 12-Step Meetings for Family Members

Sample "Wish List"

- Cake decorating
- Conversational French
- Political Science
- Business & organization
- Dog training
- Studio Art
- World History
- American Popular Culture
- Philosophy

Interpreting Results

The list generated in the first part of the exercise indicates the variety of training and experiences someone already has at their disposal for application in the production dramaturg's world. Surprisingly, many of the tools we acquire from our daily lived experiences relate to theatrical productions in quite remarkable ways. Here are a few examples:

1. The knowledge of stock car and sprint car racing customs enabled a production dramaturg to come to the table with ideas regarding how the director and scenic designer could apply these cultural phenomena to the visual design of the world of the play.

2. Courses in world religions reminded the production dramaturg for *Our Town* of the potential Buddhist underpinnings to the text and encouraged her to re-examine the play's manipulation of time.

3. The recollection of attending 12-Step Program meetings with her family when her brother was in rehabilitation prompted new play dramaturg to suggest a 12-Step meeting as a setting for a piece consisting of seemingly unconnected monologues.

The "Wish List" should not prompt anyone to suddenly enroll in more coursework or participate in activities for which there is no time. Rather, it points to the variety of content and methodologies already in a person's proverbial bag of tricks. For example, the production dramaturg for a feminist production of *The Tempest* found herself trapped in a lecture geared toward aspiring female college administrators. She "perked up" when the keynote speaker mentioned a business and organization development text that addressed gender and power. The text ultimately provided a structure for the examination of the world of the play, one completely in keeping with the director's casting and overall vision for the production.

So You Want to Be a Production Dramaturg

Before leaving this section we should note that much, if not all, of what we suggest in *The Process of Dramaturgy* is contingent on the comfort level of the director, writer and even producer. Again, though we address personal qualities and faculties that are common to sense-making processes at the heart of directing, designing, developing educational resources, and producing public relations materials, we argue that these processes are unquestionably *enhanced* by an individual concerned primarily with story management and overall continuity—in this case, the production dramaturg.

Chapter Glossary

Concept: an assortment of ideas, impressions, and theories—visual or otherwise—drawn from the story of the play by the director, which is ultimately used as an artistic jumping-off point in the creative-collaborative process.

Denis Diderot: French philosopher and writer during the Enlightenment Era best known for his *Encyclopédie*; also wrote bourgeois dramas that were accompanied by essays regarding theatrical theory and practice.

Form: the play as written; the way a play looks on the page (as opposed to style).

Gotthold Ephraim Lessing: German poet, philosopher and critic during the Enlightenment Era who was the resident critic at the Hamburg Theatre. His *Laocoon* and *The Hamburg Dramaturgy* are believed to be the roots of current dramaturgical practice in Western theatre.

Live performance event: the entire performance experience from the moment spectators enter the lobby of the theatre until they leave after the final bow.

Pre-Production: the planning phrase of a production before it goes into rehearsal; varies in organization and duration from venue to venue.

Production team: the collaborative group charged with moving a play text from the page to the stage, most often the director, light designer, sound designer, set designer, costume designer, production dramaturg, and stage manager.

Style of production: the manner in which thematic concerns manifest themselves visually and orally onstage; the way a play looks on stage in production (as opposed to form); examples include

Expressionism, Symbolism, Constructivism, Post-Modernism, Representational Realism and the like; "The concept [car] drives the style of production."

Thematic concerns: messages, as opposed to a monolithic meaning, contained within the written text that shape the world of the play both in form and in style.

Unified production: ultimate goal of the production team; all elements (directing, acting, scene design, costume design, lighting, sound, etc.) strive to compliment and support one another, working together to affect spectators in a way that upholds the concept.

PART ONE
Pre-Production

In this section we focus on a multiplicity of preparatory endeavors production dramaturgs often tackle as they work toward the first read-through of the play text. For those readers who come to this book more experienced in regards to the machinations of (and expectations for) theatre and live performance, much of what we discuss will be familiar though reframed to fit the role of production dramaturg. For those who come to this book with little understanding of theatre and live performance beyond what they have seen on stage, these chapters serve as an accessible introduction to what happens "behind the scenes" in preparation for rehearsals, with an obvious focus on the tasks of the production dramaturg. In either case, we use Part One to outline a way to arrive at what scholar, playwright and dramaturg Leon Katz refers to as the production dramaturg's "exquisite sensibility" of knowing what to say and when to say it.

Moving from collecting research materials, to contacting a director and on to deciding whether or not a theoretical framework will aid in clarifying production choices, these first three chapters progress sequentially to provide a foundation for a production dramaturg's "exquisite sensibility" when preparing for the rehearsal process. The hazard in offering any type of chronology, of course, is that it shrouds the idiosyncratic nature of collaboration and makes the pre-production preparation process look and sound like it is rather orderly and precise, which we find is scarcely the case. It is a useful approach here, however, in that it allows us to take a closer look at common preparations for the rehearsal process.

Chapter One

Laying the Groundwork

This chapter argues that the research skills, creativity and inventiveness needed to tackle diverse production dramaturgical processes—whether researching production history, applying literary theory to a classic play, tracing the antecedent of a Broadway musical, or working on new material with a living writer—all stem from solid preparation. Later we will talk about how these elements overlap, converge or diverge in interesting ways. Like any member of the production team, the production dramaturg begins by reading the play, performing acts of text analysis, developing initial impressions, and responding and reacting to the piece. However, the production dramaturg, whenever possible, begins the investigative process much earlier than the other participants in the production. Ultimately, the production dramaturg must be intellectually available to the director early on in the process, must be on hand to provide designers with insights and background material not already gathered, must take the lead in the preparation of resource packs for the cast (and director) while at the same time compiling the basic units of the production book, and much, much more.

The Production Book

The **production dramaturg's "book"** is unlike the stage manager's prompt material or the director's tome in that it may or may not include a copy of the play text or encompass blocking and cues. It is also different in that it serves as the onsite repository of vital production information. Moreover, it differs from the stage manager's book in that it is difficult to effectively compile production-viable information without thoroughly parsing the text at hand. As common sense suggests, every production poses its own unique set of questions, so the content of production dramaturgy books vary widely. This said, in our own work we have come to recognize several common elements in preparing a book for rehearsals. These include:

- A glossary of terms and concepts (See **The Gloss** below.)
- Notes on the play's production history (influential productions with performance reviews)
- A compilation of pertinent socio-cultural information (perhaps including a time-line)
- Playwright information
- History/**Historiography**
- Dramatic Criticism/Commentary
- Images of art, architecture, geography, and the like as referenced within the play text
- Often, a scene break down
- Notes on **genre**
- Pertinent notes on characters (their specific functions in the machinations of the play)

The production dramaturg's book, of course, continues to evolve throughout the planning and production process—sometimes growing in size while at other times contracting as the director takes a different tack and dramaturgy materials are shed to match. Recently, a first-time student production dramaturg was dismayed when, at the opening design meeting, collaborators asked for information not in the preparatory materials. Self-identified as an actor with a love for research, and perfectionist by nature, the production dramaturg had dutifully met with the director over the course of several months. Based both on isolated research and director-dramaturg conversations the production dramaturg had compiled quite a hefty production dramaturgy book, typed and with tabs. What was experienced in that moment, though, was the transitory, process-oriented, evolutionary nature of production dramaturgy—the continual feelings of "finding" and sometimes "letting go" in which those of us engaged in dramaturgical work revel. After viewing a couple of production dramaturg notebooks that had been ravaged by use at rehearsals, the first-time production dramaturg was able to re-engage in the process, seek answers to the designers' questions, and recapture a feeling of satisfaction from completing assigned dramaturgical tasks.

In what follows we explore the early phases of production dramaturgical inquiry—the sometimes solo archival work, the reading and preparation for early meetings with the director, and much of the **"hunting and gathering"** that many people unfamiliar with dramaturgy believe is the production dramaturg's sole function. Of course, all members of a production team "hunt and gather." It is, however, the level to which the production dramaturg engages in this process and the critical lenses employed that sets them apart from other members of the artistic team. As we examine the practical skills necessary for production dramaturgy and provide models and examples, remember that the production dramaturg's tasks are intertwined and dialectical in the ways in which practical considerations speak to creative interpretation and vice versa. This is no different from the way in which directors balance aesthetics with exigencies of casting or the way designers acknowledge pragmatics of space and budget as each pursues artistic goals. The production dramaturg's work is active, collaborative and driven by preparation, all of which begins with an intimate acquaintance with the play text at hand. To forge that relationship, then we begin with some of the "nuts and bolts" of the production dramaturgy book.

While we advocate breadth in the tasks undertaken by a singular production dramaturg, we appreciate that in different venues it might be beneficial to create dramaturgical teams, dividing the tasks between two or more individuals. In some academic settings, it might even be profitable to teach dramaturgy by having a production dramaturgy class take on the responsibilities as a whole. Dependent upon the degree of critical sophistication, of course, a supervising dramaturg may well parcel out "hunting and gathering" to learners but reserve the critical interpretation of gathered material for themselves. Whatever the case may be, we begin our discussion of pre-production preparation by addressing techniques and tools involved with hunting, gathering, and organizing.

The Gloss

Though perhaps not the first intuitive encounter with the play text, one of the production dramaturg's requisite assignments is the compilation of a "Glossary of Terms and Concepts" for use in the **production resource packet**. This deceptively simple task entails some decision-making with regard to not only the selection of items from the script that should be included but also the level at which to "pitch" the glossary itself. Textual idiosyncrasies influence the selection process, but there are some basic principles to which the production dramaturg should adhere. Since the glossary itself will be included in the production resource packet and parts of it may appear in **study guides** for special events like school matinees, the material written and compiled should be pitched at approximately an eighth grade reading level. This benchmark, which is used by several newspaper publishers, ensures a readable list that not only offers production-relevant definitions but also identifies expressions that may be unfamiliar to individuals due to geographic or cultural limitations.

To begin construction of the glossary, a production dramaturg often highlights words in the play text, compiles a full list, and cross-references two or three sources before assigning meaning(s). As expected, a more experienced production dramaturg can multi-task the way through even the first reading of a text, making notes on other aspects of the play while also identifying items for the glossary. What exactly to include in such a list? We have found that it is generally helpful to incorporate the following kinds of information:

- Proper Names/Nouns (People, Places, Things)
- Dates mentioned in the text
- Geographical terms other than proper nouns
    (i.e. rainforest, tundra, prairie, longitude and latitude coordinates)
- Geological terms
- Technological terms, inventions, innovations
- Period lingo, jargon of any kind, and Popular Culture references

- Any sorts of discipline-specific terminology
  (i.e. mathematical equations, foreign language words or
  phrases, psychological terminology, and the like)
- Flora, fauna, and the natural world

It is also wise to carefully parse the play's title. Sometimes a name is just a name and sometimes it is it the key to innovation. Lorraine Hansberry's title *A Raisin in the Sun*, for example, is imbued with multiple meanings and potential connotations, given that it is derived from a Langston Hughes poem. Exploring this connection might generate some interesting visual metaphors in production. We find it is always better to be safe than sorry, and analyze the title.

Most frequently, items in the glossary are arranged alphabetically with the act, scene and page (or line number) on which each appears noted in some fashion. Needless to say, there is no hard and fast set of rules when crafting the glossary of terms and concepts. Perhaps it is advantageous to arrange words by topic. Maybe it makes more sense to list the words in order of appearance in the play text. Perhaps it might even be necessary to blend styles and approaches to this particular task in order to best fit the requirements of a given production. Whatever the case may be, what is most important is that anyone who picks up the glossary, especially the director and performers, be able to quickly and easily find the term or concept within the play text.

Before proceeding to other aspects of the "hunting and gathering" phase, we thought it might be helpful to offer some glossary excerpts to get a better sense of what is useful to include. Take note of how each production dramaturg chose to arrange glossary material. In reviewing the examples, refer to the list of information above regarding what to consider including in the "hunting and gathering" process, to see how the particular words or concepts selected fall into the suggested categories.

Eric Overmyer's *On the Verge: Or, the Geography of Yearning* provides a special challenge to the production dramaturg because of its intermingling of both fictive and real geographic locales, ranging from the elusive "Terra Incognita" and other vague references like "mysterious interior" to quite specific geographic references like Potala. The script contains specific longitude and latitude allusions that support

SAMPLE GLOSSARY excerpt from *On the Verge, or The Geography of Yearning*
Southern Illinois University Carbondale
Anne Fletcher and Jennifer Caudell, Dramaturgical Team
Lori Merrill-Fink, Director

Page #	Term/Allusion	Meaning/Explanation
Act One		
1	Embarcadero	A landing place, esp. on an inland waterway
2	Terra Incognita	Unexplored country (or field of knowledge)
2	Peregrinations	Travelings/wanderings
2	Sartorial	Related to tailoring
2	*Pro forma cuppa*	As a matter of form, "cup of"- so, the obligatory cup of tea, perhaps
3	Sherpas	Mountain dwelling people of Nepal; Guides for climbing in the Himalayas
3	Ocarina	Wind instrument, like a recorder
3	Barley sugar	Candy made from sugar, water and barley
4	Palaver	Long parley btw. people of different cultures or classes
4	Pasha	Man of high rank (Turkish. North African)
4	Tonsorial	Of or pertaining to the work of a barber or hairdressing
6	*Qu-est ce que c'est?*	What is it? (French)

the playwright's tongue-in-cheek (and remarkably brilliant) approach to both the "geography" and "yearning" to which he alludes in his title. *On the Verge's* peregrinations across time and place with specific popular culture references make it a test of the production dramaturg's skills and patience.

This type of challenge is not reserved, however, for contemporary language-based plays like those of Overmyer. In fact, classic play texts often come with their own special set of difficulties when considering the compilation of a glossary of terms and concepts. Not only must the production dramaturg pay special attention to obscure puns and word play but also must account for issues of translation, whether Greek, Italian or Latin.

SAMPLE GLOSSARY excerpt from *Titus Andronicus*
Illinois Shakespeare Festival
Scott R. Irelan, Production Dramaturg
Catherine Weidner, Director

Gratify (4.2.12): honor; grace

Grey (2.2.1): early daylight, before sunrise; Sky-blue

Ground (2.1.70): foundation; bass in music

Hie (3.1.285): hasten

Honey-stalks (4.4.80): clover

Horning (2.3.67): cuckolding your husband

Insinuate (4.2.38): flatter

Insult on (3.2.71): triumph over

"'Integer vitae, scelerisque purus,/Non eget Mauri jaculis, nec arcu'" (4.2.20-1) : the opening lines of Horace's *Odes* –"The man who is of pure life and free from crime needs not the arrows or the bow of the Moor"

Kind (1.1.61): attached by natural affection

Lascivious Goth (2.3.110): homophobic pun on Goth/goat; goats were lascivious

Like a churl (1.1.488): so rudely

Love day (1.1.493): a day for friendly settling of disputes

We should mention that while some might consider glossing a Shakespeare text a futile endeavor, there are three practical reasons providing a glossary for these play texts has proven vital to our professional work. First, professional companies do not always work from a published edition with footnotes (i.e. Arden or Folger). Rather, they often use electronic copies that have cuts, adjustments in language and the like, complete with re-pagination and re-lining (mentioned in Chapter Four). Second, the glossary process allows a production dramaturg to consult at least three sources, including the *Oxford English Dictionary*, in order to find the best contextual meaning. Lastly, and perhaps most significant, we find that the creation of a glossary on such a text is a productive way to enhance careful study of the text, study which leads to much richer acts of dramaturgy as the rehearsal process moves toward opening night.

Production History

Another factor for the production dramaturg to consider during this early phase of preparation is outlining **production history**. Like developing the glossary, this endeavor requires a production dramaturg to decide not only what segment(s) of a given production's history are included and excluded, but also how much or how little to cover. To some extent, this decision-making is either aided or hindered, most times, by three main external factors. These are in no particular order: 1) the popularity or obscurity of the live performance event; 2) the pervasiveness of print within the culture in which a show is produced; and 3) the ease of accessing print materials whether in hard copy or from an online database.

While perhaps an obvious statement, the production dramaturg should start with the premiere not only because it is quite a good place to start but also because writings regarding the first live performance event may guide a production dramaturg to performances of note in subsequent years. Apart from this, it is necessary to look for material referencing the most recent production. It is from within these two extremes that a production dramaturg can amass a well-rounded production history. We have found that spending time identifying influential productions and collecting as many performance reviews as possible regarding these productions to be the most beneficial approach.

The filtering process may yield as little as one account of a live performance event or as many as fifteen or twenty. It is also a good idea to see if there are any well-received film adaptations, as with *My Fair Lady* or *A Christmas Carol*, for example. Although film versions often bear little resemblance to a given play text in performance, the general public may be more familiar with the mediatized rendering than the live performance version. In addition, a production dramaturg should take note of both where each performance response was published and the name of the writer. Often these two pieces of information can illuminate why a particular production review narrative was positive or negative. No matter what the publication venue, it is useful to make note of the following types of commonalities and differences, gaps and repetitions between and among review publications:

- Producers, designers, directors, and performers
- Design choices whether sound, lighting, costume, prop, or scenic
- Educational, non-profit, for-profit venues
- Dates of production
- Length of run and reasons for closing
- National tour or International tour
- Move from Off-Off Broadway or Off-Broadway to Broadway venue
- East coast, west coast, or Canadian premiere or revival
- Adaptation to film, ice show or other performance type
- Adaptation from antecedent source (i.e. book, foreign language novella)

We should point out that at this groundwork stage, production dramaturgs do not necessarily draw any conclusions from the assorted production history narratives. Instead, they simply make notes for further research, which is usually not undertaken until after first contact with the director. Furthermore, there may be scholarly articles available that have done much of the initial work of identifying influential productions. These are easily accessed through databases such as JSTOR or *Project Muse*. Of course working on the premier production of a new work is a different story as is researching an early modern text since there would not necessarily be articles or reviews on the inaugural production of either of these. In the case of a play text that has little or no production history—like those of the early modern period—it is always a good idea to look for popular press articles or scholarly essays that write about the play-in-production, making note of stagings now considered influential to contemporary live performance events.

We talk in much more detail about the shift from laying the ground-work to developing a dramaturgical sensibility in regards to this type of information within Chapter Two and Chapter Three. Ultimately, while exploration of production history is vital to the production dramaturg's understanding of the written text in live performance, use of information beyond this varies from venue to venue, production to production. In many cases what is used as an educational tool by directors for performers in academic settings is not necessarily relevant or appropriate in a professional environment.

Sociocultural Information

Because the production history is a finite resource that largely considers elements experienced during a situated live performance event, it is important for a production dramaturg to get a quick sense of what was happening within both global society and popular culture at the time the show opened. It may also prove rewarding to pull together this type of information for each of the production history narratives reviewed. There is some validity in a production dramaturg creating a timeline of events so that the director, performers, and designers alike can see what might have had direct influence not only on the play text but also the performance text at any given time. We have found it constructive to keep track of the following when generating a cursory understanding of a particular sociocultural landscape:

- Science, Industry, and Technological Innovations
- Philosophy
- Art, Furniture, and Architecture
- Popular print media (i.e. editorial cartoons or novels)
- Dance, Visual Art, Opera, Operetta
- Wars and skirmishes
- Treaties and trade agreements

- Social welfare programs and census data
- Maps and Topography

The aforementioned information, which is by no means an exhaustive list, purposefully seizes upon obvious points of interest because at the "hunt and gather" level of work a production dramaturg need not be consumed by historiography largely because it may or may not be useful to the director. However, when the director (and production design team) is clearer on their intention for the production, then the production dramaturg must turn to history and historiographic inquiry to best develop a research perspective that will be relevant to the final production.

Playwright Background

The last obligatory portion of groundwork is gathering some basic understanding of the playwright. This is important for two reasons. First, because plays are produced at a situated time and place, it is always advisable to conjecture, based on available evidence, why the play was drafted by a writer for a certain spectatorship at a specific time for a particular venue. Second, similar to the parsing of character names and titles, being acquainted with what a playwright embraces or rejects can lead a production dramaturg to keys to unlocking metaphors, themes, and motifs within a given text. We have found it quite informative to note the following when gathering background on a playwright:

- Self-identification markers such as age, gender, race, and sex
- Childhood data (i.e. parents' class status, first job, etcetera)
- Education level, place of education, general content area
- First publication whether a play text or not
- Underlying artistic philosophy (i.e. August Wilson and the **4 B's**)
- Political bent and lobbying efforts (i.e. Liberal Democrat and Greenpeace)
- Life partner status (i.e. married, widowed, divorced, single for life)
- Hobbies and non-writing endeavors (i.e. kayaking, history buff)

Again, at this point in the process it is not necessary to draw any inferences vis-à-vis the play text in question. Naturally, those who are more practiced at this phase of work or more familiar with a particular writer and their work may immediately be able to make connections between writer and text. Whatever the case, a basic understanding of "who, what, when, where, why, and to what extent" in regards to the life and times of a writer are indispensable to the production dramaturg. Of course, retrospectively, playwrights' works are often categorized in phases or within genre limitations (writing only comedies for example), and these thematic concerns often reverberate across a writer's body of work. This, too, is important information to seek out. The four categories of information mentioned thus far are vital to production resource packets, which should be made available shortly after casting is complete. Naturally, the director will be intimately involved in the selection of materials for inclusion in these packets and might provide specific inspirational items, but both the task of gathering an array to show the director and assembling the information for easy distribution to the company most frequently falls to the production dramaturg. The four categories of information mentioned thus far are vital to production resource packets that, whenever possible, should be made available shortly after casting is complete. This information is also often quite useful to the **table work** portion of rehearsals.

A production dramaturg armed with this type of foundational information is now better prepared to open a dialogue with the director (discussed in Chapter Two). Based in part on the way the first discussion progresses and the focus the director gives to various elements, the production's research agenda will take shape and become much more focused. We have found that often our advanced work takes us further into the following realms:

- History/Historiography
- Dramatic Criticism/Commentary
- Inspiration images (for designers largely)
- Often, a scene breakdown
- Pertinent notes on characters
  their specific functions in the machinations of the play
- Miscellaneous directorial requests

- Eventually, specific notes related to the director's overall **production concept**

The dramaturg's production book creates categories of information from which to launch an intellectually stimulating and aesthetically pleasing creative-collaborative process. Without a foundational sense of terms and concepts, production history, probable sociocultural influences, and playwright background, the production dramaturg cannot fully engage in the advanced research work that comes with developing and maintaining an intellectually challenging and aesthetically pleasing rapport with the director and, ultimately, a unified production. It is crucial to remember that, whether beginner or seasoned vet, the production dramaturg has much to offer not only a respective production team but also the larger community in which the theatre resides when committing "acts of dramaturgy" at any given venue.

So You Want to Be a Production Dramaturg

Information gathering, of course, revolves around a variety of sources. The sources themselves appear in a range of forms. As the production dramaturg prepares to meet with the director it is probably best to begin scouring general sources before pursuing a specialized agenda. Specificity and focus, in practice, are often inspired by the director's vision. As we close this chapter on "hunting and gathering" we thought it appropriate to provide a listing of some valuable resources for groundwork. This is by no means an exhaustive list. For some working in academic environments, this is the first and last phase of work to be done. For others, it is the inception of a long and winding road to opening night. In either case, we are sure that these resources will prove helpful. Of course it goes without saying that no matter what level or depth of information is found and generated, full citation of source material is a must.

An Exercise on Preparing: Sourcing the Show

Developed by Southern Illinois University Carbondale instructor Randall Colburn as an in-class exercise for his survey course, this exercise asks the hypothetical production dramaturg to reflect on possible research paths for an imagined production of a play about two warring churches in downtown Chicago in the 1950s.

Instructions

1. Reflect upon the research categories necessary to prepare for the first meeting with your director.

2. Consider the most relevant religious, political and material sources to which you could turn. Are there significant primary sources you could utilize? People, places, or things?

3. List the five best sources you find, annotating them via their relevant connection to 1950s Chicago.

Chapter Glossary

Production Resource Packet: a specific collection of information taken from the production dramaturg's book that specifically addresses issues, images and insights needed by collaborators as they prepare for the live performance event

4 B's: Amiri Baraka, Romare Beardon, the Blues, and Jorge Luis Borges; the four overriding influences on August Wilson's dramatic form and style.

Genre: French for type or kind in this case when referring to play scripts

Historiography: Briefly, the study of the study of history; looking at history or a given moment in history not as "fact" but as an amalgamation of ideas that converge at that given moment, each influencing the other; recognizing that historians bring to their world views their own sets of "baggage" and interpret the past through their respective idiosyncratic lenses

"Hunting and Gathering": The act of assembling research material pertinent to the production, begun prior to first meeting with the director and executed during the pre-production phase.

Production Concept: the guiding vision for a live performance event as provided by the director

Production History: The (chronological) list of major productions of any given play from its initial performance to the present. Often patterns of interpretative style can be ascertained by an examination of a play's production history.

Production dramaturg's "book": The dramaturg's more extensive notebook containing information pertinent to the production, sometimes given over to the director or stage manager as a reference guide during the rehearsal process. This is sometimes referred to as a casebook or protocol.

Study Guides: outreach materials provided most often to educators as they prepare a population of learners for engaging with a live performance event. These can include lesson plans, suggested reading lists, and critical essay material among other components.

Table work: a rehearsal technique in which the director, production dramaturg, and actors literally sit around a table and read the play, discussing issues, rhythm, language, social context and the like

Chapter Two

Opening a Dialogue

This second chapter reflects upon the production dramaturg's next all-important question, "Now what?" That is, we direct our attention away from simply "hunting and gathering" and toward interpreting accumulated information in preparation for initial pre-production (perhaps even pre-casting) conversations with the director. Not unlike the "Taking Stock" exercise at the end of the Introduction, this is a moment in the process where a production dramaturg should take time to consider what might be of most benefit to an introductory discussion (or two) focused on discovering the director's production intention.

Unfortunately, many educational and professional theatre producers still do not see the validity in making a move into this phase of committing acts of dramaturgy—a shift which inherently nudges the production dramaturg away from merely "hunting and gathering" and toward a winding path of communication regarding innovation and inspiration. Innovation and inspiration are, after all, at the heart of a production dramaturg's sensibility as a creative-collaborative artist. Often, production calendars are compressed or even rushed, and the production dramaturg is not brought into the process until ideas have been relatively cemented. No matter what the circumstance, though, dialogue with the artistic team is always a productive and insight-filled act of dramaturgy.

Setting Some Ground Rules

The production dramaturg is most useful to creative-collaboration when considered an essential member of the artistic team. In this case, notions of continuity also extend into the working relationship a production dramaturg has with a producing organization (or director). One of the most important issues to resolve early is the extent to which the production dramaturg will be a presence during rehearsal sessions. It is equally important to agree on how early that presence will be established. This is essential when negotiating ground rules in both academic and professional environments because the difference between being a production dramaturg and being just a researcher is the time spent in creative-collaboration with directors, designers, producers and the rest of the artistic team. It is also wise to make attendance at production meetings part of the larger agreement. This is especially of concern in venues that do not have a full-time production dramaturg because it might not always occur to the production manager to include the production dramaturg on a meeting request. We should mention, too, that it is sometimes difficult to explain to designers and technicians why a production dramaturg needs to be at these meetings at all. In fact, a production dramaturg should request that the director do the explaining so as not to appear to be the "history police" or "concept police", which many design collaborators will "write off" as one more person giving them notes they do not necessarily want or need.

Our experiences suggest that the earlier production dramaturgs are brought into the process and the more often they are a part of each meeting and rehearsal session, the more effective they will be in not only monitoring continuity but also influencing decision-making. This, however, is not always feasible. Sometimes the director wants a fresh set of eyes, so being at every rehearsal runs counter to that strategy. At times, the production dramaturg may be working on multiple shows at once, which precludes them from frequent attendance. Perhaps the dramaturg position is unpaid and there is no financial incentive to be present at a good number of meetings or sessions. In any event, the Literary Managers and Dramaturgs of America (LMDA) provide some helpful (and rather extensive) employment guidelines for members and non-members alike on the association website [www.lmda.org].

Unlike **Actor's Equity** or **IATSE**, LMDA cannot collectively bargain for members. The organization does, however, offer advocacy for members as they negotiate agreements for service. In this capacity, LMDA suggests that a freelance production dramaturg attend half of the rehearsals and, in turn, receive half the compensation of the director. Of course, with six recognized categories of employment—ranging from resident production dramaturg at an established regional theatre to staffer at a new play development house or summer Shakespeare festival—the pay scale fluctuates too.[1] Admittedly there is rarely a copious amount of money to be had as a production dramaturg, so obtaining a **letter of agreement** (or full contract) is much more about clarifying expectations than anything else. Moreover, beginning production dramaturgs will most likely need to hone, if not prove, skills in a professional internship or post-baccalaureate apprenticeship before achieving the "cultural capital" needed when negotiating monetary specifics. Whatever the case may be, it is imperative that no matter how much an individual is being paid or what the job on a specific production is defined to be, the production dramaturg has to take themselves seriously as a professional. In the end, coming to some sort of consensus about the depth and breadth of involvement is not only vital to a productive creative-collaborative experience but also imperative to avoiding the pitfalls of doing (or saying) either too much or not enough within a given context.

Time to Start Thinking Like a Production Dramaturg

One of the most remarkable challenges a production dramaturg can experience is shifting both mentally and artistically from assembling **primary** and **secondary source material** (and abridging the corresponding information) to deciphering and decoding that material

---

1   Six categories of Employment: 1) Staff dramaturg/literary manager hired by not-for-profit institution or for-profit institution/producer; 2) Freelance production dramaturg hired by not-for-profit or commercial producer; 3) Freelance production dramaturg hired by playwright; 4) Freelance production dramaturg hired by director; 5) Dramaturg at universities/colleges; and 6) Dramaturg/literary manager on staff or free-lance at new play development center in which no full productions are presented.

in such a way that will be of benefit to the director, the larger production staff and, later, the cast. Having spent so much time in the
archives, or investigating online databases, or browsing the pages of
Playbill, the production dramaturg must pause and consciously modify
day-to-day work so as to begin taking a long view of what the live
performance event might become, how it will arrive with all elements
working together and what outreach and public relations might do for
unified storytelling. Of course, in the name of continuity, this does not
necessarily mean that the cerebral functions outlined in Chapter One
are shut off altogether. It is, in fact, at the juncture of relevant research
and attentive application where a dramaturgical sensibility lies. Most
frequently the production dramaturg arrives at this juncture through
dialogue with the director. As the director selects from the smorgasbord of material offered, the production dramaturg is prompted to
refine and/or continue research. We explore this more completely in
Chapter Four.

Making Contact

Some of the most important conversations a production dramaturg can and will have are the first few times "talking shop" with the
director. Even so, production dramaturgs, no matter what level of expertise and practice, will have their fair share of awkward, or perhaps,
problematic sessions with a director. We certainly have. Indeed, while
there are many directors who fully enlist a production dramaturg as
a sounding board and creative-collaborative colleague—sharing ideas,
opinions and hurdles to overcome with the production at hand—some
feel threatened by the mere presence of a production dramaturg, irra-
tionally thinking that this collaborator is determined from the outset
to ruin the "concept" or that the production dramaturg is a frustrated
director trying to work an angle. Others may not have any idea how
to use the materials generated during the initial research process and
ask for nothing more than the resource material discussed in Chapter
One. Still others may ask the production dramaturg to fetch them coffee and a donut with sprinkles because the director had no training
whatsoever, formal or otherwise, on how best to engage a production
dramaturg as a creative-collaborator with beneficial insights.

For example, a large state university decides to produce *Nickel and Dimed* by Joan Holden—an adaptation of Barbara Ehrenreich's *Nickel and Dimed, on (Not) Getting by in America*—as part of a season about social justice. Epic in style and quick in pace, the play recounts Ehrenreich's first person description of her journey through a series of low wage jobs at fictionalized places like Kenny's Restaurant, Magic Maids cleaning service and Mall-Mart. Given this content a faculty member comes up with what appears to be a superb outreach effort to coincide with a preview night performance—inviting all of the unionized campus laborers, such as custodial staff and pipe fitters, to attend the production for free. The production dramaturg mentions to the director that both Ehrenreich and Holden make it quite clear that their narrative is directed at upper middle class individuals (like a university president and the cabinet of vice presidents) and not those in hourly positions. The faculty member presses the issue and wins because, in the end, the director is more concerned with having spectators in attendance that reflect personages in the play than continuity with stated writerly intent. The point here is that when thinking as production dramaturg, it is important to pay attention to the worries, warnings and wants revealed by production reviews, playwright interviews and all other background material generated in the "hunt and gather" phase. Objections phrased with "The playwright/ adaptor says…" statements can be a non-threatening way for a production dramaturg to voice thoughts and concerns to their director. These assertions, however, are often disregarded if the dramaturg-director relationship is not one of honest communication, trust and creative-collaboration. We continue this chapter, then, by considering ways in which the production dramaturg might effectively go about establishing a strong, open line of communication with a director prior to the first rehearsal session.

Ideally the final agreement of terms between a producing organization and the production dramaturg will be established before making the first phone call or sending an introductory email to the director. If this is indeed the case, then the initial contact should be spent outlining elements of that agreement as well as actively listening to how the director prefers to engage a production dramaturg in the rehearsal and staging process. The reality is that most production dramaturgs are negotiating boundaries with the producing organization and the director in tandem, if not in reverse. In either situation, some important things to spell out with the director include: 1) the percentage/number of rehearsals to be attended; 2) the types of information to be included in the production resource pack and ways in which the director would like overall research to proceed; and 3) the way that notes are to be relayed to performers and other members of the artistic team. We should note that this final point can be drastically different in academic settings as opposed to those of the professional theatre world. In our professional collaborations, notes have only ever gone from the production dramaturg to the director. On a new play project notes have gone to both the playwright and the director. We have never sent notes directly to a performer or a designer without the director's consent because it is highly inappropriate to do so in most situations.[2] In addition, the only direct contact we have had with designers is on research questions, many of which are handled within production meetings. Whatever the channel of communication, directors are included in all correspondence. In academic settings, however, the channels of communication and rules of decorum frequently call for some direct contact with student collaborators over term breaks, holiday recess or summer vacation, for example, in order to better facilitate active learning.

In instances where the director feels ill at ease with certain elements of an agreement between the company and a production dramaturg, the artistic director or managing director should be contacted. Many differences are minor and easily remedied (i.e. percentage/number of rehearsals attended) while others will prove more problematic (i.e. distrust of production dramaturgy and the production dramaturg in general). Be aware, too, that if the production dramaturg is working with a director who is unfamiliar with any previous dramaturgical work, the director may use this first contact to get a sense of how supportive or contrary the production dramaturg may well be in rehearsals. In all cases, this initial communication is a time for the production drama-

---

2   In some creative-collaborative environments, like that of Western Theatre Conspiracy in Vancouver and their *Live from a Bush of Ghosts*, the production dramaturg often has more flexibility when interacting with performers, directly offering storytelling notes and continuity comments.

turg to listen and ask "What if?" questions in order to ascertain how to best assist the director in planning for the rehearsal process.

Regardless of whether a production dramaturg has ever worked with a particular director before, once initial contact has been established and parameters for the dramaturg's contributions have been set, the simple act of writing a letter to the director—or in this age a professional email—is both a non-threatening and constructive way to expand established lines of communication. In this letter the production dramaturg can further outline the information already gathered, go about suggesting production pitfalls to avoid (garnered from personal experience with a particular play in performance or from accounts and reviews of past productions), propose insights regarding the script (**theme, metaphor, spine**), and indicate recurring patterns that develop in reviewing the groundwork material. It is a good idea to think of this document as a cover letter of sorts for the dramaturgy production book and subsequent production resource materials. This said, the production dramaturg may elect to send just the letter itself, saving the production book material for a face-to-face meeting. Once again, at this point in the process there are no hard and fast rules or established protocol, per se. It is essential, however, to always get a sense of what the director might appreciate more. What we often find, too, is that portions of this letter can, and inevitably will, serve as the foundation for talking points (discussed later in this chapter). It is interesting to note that talking points are frequently folded into a pre-show audience discussion or even the program notes. Even so, if the production dramaturg senses some creative-collaborative unease from the director, then it is probably wise to leave some of the below suggested information out of the letter in favor of using it later, in person, as talking points. The last thing the production dramaturg wants to do is overwhelm a director with an excess of ideas and materials too soon in the preparation process. This may well be the first time a production dramaturg insinuates a questioning spirit into the production process, so make it count. However, be careful not to alienate the director. Keep in mind that part of the production dramaturg's job is to open up a safe space for discourse. If the production dramaturg loses the director before a bulk of production meetings even start, then it is difficult to be utilized as fully as possible over the course of the rehearsal process.

An Exercise on Dialoguing

Crafting a "Letter to the Director"

Adapted from ideas mentioned by Mark Bly at the 1994 LMDA conference[3], this "Letter to the Director" exercise was first used as part of an in-class session focused on dialoguing with hesitant or resistant directors and has since become part of a larger unit that asks student production dramaturgs to use the letter as a tool to get pressing thoughts in order before talking with a director. This letter is most appropriately given or sent to the director after initial contact establishes some basic elements the director is interested in pursuing and the production dramaturg revises the material to match these interests. Admittedly, in our professional practice this type of dialogue often happens through a succession of email messages and phone conversations rather than a formal letter, per se. This is, in part, because creative-collaborators in the professional ranks have to juggle several projects at once and the ability to do this type of idea-generating in quick bursts is a must. However, as the below examples indicate, collecting our thoughts in these categories remains a part of our professional practice and often shapes the contact we make with a director.

Instructions

Thinking back over the information collected so far and your reactions to the written text, write a letter to the director using a modified five paragraph format. There will be plenty of time to expand on these ideas at a later time.

This is an interpretation of what was found while compiling the glossary, located within production histories, and assembled from relevant sociocultural information. Make sure to point to connections between what was found and the director's proclivities.

Paragraph Break Down

- "I see…"
- Milieu
- Text and production history/what to avoid and what to be aware of when working (if applicable)

---

3   Mark Bly, "Bristling with Possibilities." In *Dramaturgy in American Theater: A Sourcebook*. Ed. Susan Jonas et al. (New York: Harcourt Brace College Publishers, 1997) 50.

- Considerations for staging moment and/or innovation
- Close with "for me" statements...

If nothing else use this letter as a way of connecting the play text and eventual live performance event with the larger social/cultural world in which you live and work.

Expanding and Explicating

The first paragraph should open with some sort of "I see" statement that indicates a strong point of view. Think of it as an opening position statement in a light-hearted debate of ideas for which the rest of the letter will argue. For some productions it may be necessary to go into great detail in order to provide a background for assertions. Yet some productions may only need a few sentences of introduction both to establish and to defend a particular perspective. Regardless of how long or short, the first paragraph should always include the "I see" statement as its first sentence and a review of what is to come in the following sections of the letter. This format not only serves as a synopsis of the piece but also presents ideas from a non-threatening, situated perspective.

Sample First Paragraph from *My Fair Lady* Letter to the Director
McLeod Summer Playhouse
Scott R. Irelan, Production Dramaturg
J. Thomas Kidd, Director

I see a musical about modernization, urbanization, economic progression, and intense industrialization. One of the most interesting layers provided by Shaw's play text that seems to be lost in the translation from page to stage is that the original play dealt heavily with the struggle for equality and identity in a transitional world that was moving from agrarian/pastoral to urban/metropolitan. Shaw amassed several "non-play" writings, which indicated his desire for more cultural sensitivity and less class distinction while also haranguing the residue of aristocratic influences and elitist ignorance in relation to the poorest of the poor. What follows are some personal connections to the cultural milieu of Shaw and his *Pygmalion*, thoughts on the variety of musical scores available for production from

Tams-Witmark, and, finally, suggestions for ways to combat the monolith that is *My Fair Lady* based on our previous conversation regarding all three.

The second paragraph should address milieu. What this entails exactly, as might be expected, changes from script to script. In most cases this will be information about the context in which the play text was first written and produced. These "roots" often lead the production dramaturg to suggest ways of bridging then and now. If working on an adaptation, translation, or musical, then this paragraph may need to discuss the antecedant(s) and the respective social energy. If it is a new play in development, then this paragraph may need to examine not only the milieu of the **world of the play** but also that of the present day to propose how each might engage the other in ways that strengthen the story being told. In any event, it is necessary to distill this milieu information into "nuggets" that can be somehow realized in production. For example, when working on *My Fair Lady* it is imperative to look back to George Bernard Shaw and *Pygmalion* for relevant contextual cues, considering that Alan Jay Lerner's book is nearly a word for word adaptation of Shaw's play. Of course, the play's ending is drastically altered for the musical theatre-going audience to provide for the requisite "happy ending." In doing so, then, much of the sociocultural milieu discussion has no choice but to center itself on the class-based geography of London.

Milieu Excerpt from *My Fair Lady* Letter to the Director
McLeod Summer Playhouse
Scott R. Irelan, Production Dramaturg
J. Thomas Kidd, Director

Around the time Shaw penned *Pygmalion*, three distinct residential suburbs emerged: one to the east of the Thames, another to the west, and finally to the south of the river. The biggest of these was the Town of London East, which was the most poverty-stricken area of London. Even with the aid of church organizations, philanthropic endeavors and governmental intervention little "clean-up" was accomplished. To the west of the Thames there was the Village of Petersville, which was

Img. 2.1 *My Fair Lady*. McLeod Summer Playhouse. Dir.: J. Thomas Kidd. Photo: Robert Holcombe. Notice the lattice work. This was inspired by dramaturgical research into the phoenetic alphabet used by Higgins.

annexed in 1874. It became known simply as London West. The residents here were mostly city workers, or operated private gardens selling much of their produce at market. The market district officially became part of London in 1897. The most prominent name from the area is Covent Garden. Finally, the area now known as "Old South" was annexed in 1890. Located south of the river in Westminster Township this was the area where many prominent Londoners had their large estates. These massive homes where mixed in with the humble cottages of hourly wage earners. The effect was a sense of split existence. On one side of the block there could be large mansions of lawyers, doctors, and other professionals (like Higgins), while on the other pseudo-slums existed complete with ramshackle housing. The annexation of the suburbs had ceased by the beginning of WW I.

Having stated an initial impression and established relevant circumstances surrounding both writer and text, it is time to turn to the performance edition of the text being used and the production histories that have been accumulated, when applicable. If there are a variety of texts in circulation, then this is an ideal moment to share similarities and differences found between them. It also is a good time to mention which ones were seemingly received better in production.

Take care also to note whether the comments are from a world premiere, regional theatre production, college/university staging and the like. This is also the place to clearly state what reviewers, critics and academics mention as choices to avoid or problems to be aware of when tackling the production. If working on a classic play, then this might also be the place to note a desire to aid in the preparation and editing of the written text. In the end, this section of the letter should reflect upon the question: "Why this play for this audience at this time?" This logically leads, then, to a segment where ideas for staging are presented in the form of questions or prompts, not as directing or design notes.

Armed with what is known about previous attempts at the show, offer some production choices that have yet to be tried. Make sure not to limit ideas in any way. At some point budget and logistical concerns will temper the process, so there is no need to self-impose limitations at such an early stage. Consider everything from casting choices to scenic design, choreography to costumes, lobby environments to post-show exit patterns, and so on. Whatever and however this section of the letter is crafted, make certain to always have an eye on "fresh" ideas. This section need not necessarily take narrative form. We find that a numbered list or series of bullet points works just as well, if not better. In many cases this abridged format allows the director to quickly get a sense of how these ideas might manifest themselves on stage, whether implicitly or explicitly. This non-narrative formatting also lends itself to becoming a significant portion of talking points. We should note that none of the innovations mentioned on the next page appeared in the final live theatrical performance event. However, the phonetic alphabet that Higgins references was the inspiration for interlocking lattice work and intricate railings in the final scenic design (see Img. 2.1).

Innovations Excerpted from *My Fair Lady* Letter to the Director
McLeod Summer Playhouse
Scott R. Irelan, Production Dramaturg
J. Thomas Kidd, Director

- Since the play is about modernization and mechanization, could we look for ways to integrate computer technologies/ projections into the scenography? Perhaps spell out phonetically the character names, scene titles, song titles, or themes and meld them into "normal" written text on the cyc or on large open sections of wall in Higgins's place

- Should we go back to the Greek myth of Pygmalion and see if there are ways to integrate parts of that original image/ statue with current Pygmalion-eqsue images from popular culture into the set, props, projections, costuming, color palette and the like?

- Look at some of the drawn/painted renderings of the Pygmalion myth to see if you can find elements of the "laboratory of perfection" and use them as a starting point for the set pieces?

It is important to close the letter similarly to the way that it began while taking great care to illustrate that there is no overwhelming personal attachment with anything offered in the letter. It may even be essential to reiterate that the ideas presented come directly from the interests the director expressed in the first contact as well as what was discovered in the initial research process. It may also prove helpful to outline and otherwise suggest additional areas of interest that might be of use to designers, outreach and marketing. If the director seems unresponsive to receiving insights in this format, then the production dramaturg should cover the main ideas that would have been found within the letter over the phone or face-to-face through talking points. If the director is receptive to this written format, then talking points become a useful tool in furthering the exploration of ideas.

Closing Paragraph Excerpted from *My Fair Lady* Letter to the Director

McLeod Summer Playhouse
Scott R. Irelan, Production Dramaturg
J. Thomas Kidd, Director

Again, these ideas are based on my initial readings of the *My Fair Lady* text and our previous conversation. These are only suggestions regarding where to begin the process derived from what I see within the world of the musical. I have also tried to provide a few ways to "innovate" the staging. Admittedly, the scope of research still needed is beyond the limits of this material and will be expanded as we move forward in the process. However, I do hope that this has provided at least one window into a fresh approach to staging the "chestnut" that is *My Fair Lady*. I look forward to our next conversation.

Developing Talking Points

"Talking Points" are a valuable organizational tool for the production dramaturg. Prepared as a list and often arranged in bullet point fashion, these can help keep the conversation on task while, at the same time, allowing for flexibility and "in the moment" brainstorming with a director. Some directors prefer to be handed a printed copy of the talking points at the initial face-to-face meeting. Others might better digest a paragraph or two of prose that positions the written text critically, historically, socially or the like in advance of meeting. It is best to frame talking points with "I see…" observations. Additionally, personalized questions that encourage the director to state preferences, make proactive decisions and utilize the production dramaturg's work when crafting a directorial approach to the live performance event are also advantageous to creative-collaboration. It is a good idea to think about this initial stage of working with the director as offering them a smorgasbord from which will be selected items for further exploration.

Developing strong talking points requires that a production dramaturg spend substantial time reading and reflecting before creating what, at face value, appears to be quite a simple list. At this crucial juncture lie two important attributes of a production dramaturg: 1) open-minded flexibility; and 2) the ability to synthesize and make connections within the discipline, across disciplines and beyond the play text. As intimated, it is the production dramaturg's task to digest large quantities of material and process that information, making sense of it for others.

This "sense-making" step is the one where many fledgling production dramaturgs stumble. Regardless, the production dramaturg can ill afford to practice "ownership" of material when offering alternative ways of viewing a play text. Stated another way, there can be little ego-involvement in the process of brainstorming approaches because, in the end, the director makes the final decision about what is and is not appropriate for a given live performance event. Note that while the topics are wide-ranging in the *Dancing at Lughnasa* talking points example, they are presented as implied "I see..." statements. In the corresponding conversation these statements were mentioned as possible ways of seeing the text in performance. Both the director and production dramaturg were attracted to the inherent Dionysian/Apollonian binary of the play. The director, a Nigerian, was also delighted that the production dramaturg had recognized the connection to Chinua Achebe's *Things Fall Apart*. In the end, only a few of the items mentioned in this set of talking points showed up in the final production. However, the synergy provided by these talking points opened the door for a long and productive creative-collaborative relationship.

The production dramaturg needs to possess a light-hearted, questioning spirit that can be effortlessly carried into all phases of the creative-collaborative process, especially during the first few conversations with the director. Needless to say, some queries are much better than others. For example, "What part of *Titus Andronicus*, if any, do you find comedic?" may not get much mileage outside the realm of a classroom setting. But, "What if we focus on issues of family preservation and honor within *Titus Andronicus*?" might push the director toward an interesting artistic threshold while still addressing the **given circumstances** of the play. Obviously, there is no guarantee that anything that comes out of a production dramaturg's questioning will end up in the final live performance event, but the mere act of opening a spirited dialogue will forever shape the translation of a play text from the page to the stage. Whatever happens, it is the production dramaturg's obligation to "get behind" the director's vision and pursue it with tenacity.

Talking Points for *Dancing at Lughnasa*
Southern Illinois University Carbondale
Anne Fletcher, Production Dramaturg
OleSegun Ojewuyi, Director

Dionysus vs. Apollo- "Dionysus in Ballybeg" in *Friel's (Post) Colonial Drama* by F.C. McGrath

- Generalized Celtic
- Lughnasa was so important that authorities had to permit the festival to coexist w/Christianity
- Note the regenerative powers of Dionysus and the possible reasons for this thematic clash in the play- as with *The Bacchae* et al, the power of Dionysus (like the power of electricity, for example) can work both ways, for "good" or for "evil" in quotes.
- Manifestations of Dionysian in play: dance (of particular note Gerry's dancing ability), "Marconi" and its mind of its own, Father Jack and the African rituals, Gerry Evans, Danny Bradley, even the Wild Woodbines, the images on the kites, Austin Morgan (Each woman, sometimes two, has sexual desires directed at a particular man but repressed…)
- McGrath, *"The play's moral is that all people, despite a superficial civilizing exterior, are Dionysiacs. Therefore Nietzsche and Freud are as important to understanding the play as the Celtic gods."* As qtd. in Harp & Evans, p. 181
- "heathenism" needed to balance (BFE as qtd. Harp & Evans p. 459) I guess I'll have to get these, check them, and add them to Bib.

Comparisons of Friel with other playwrights, authors, etcetera

- Thornton Wilder
- Tennessee Williams
- Chekhov
- Garcia Lorca
- William Faulkner in use of fictional places with geography about them (although Friel denies this)

- O'Neill-Is not Father Jack in his regalia like the character in *A Touch of the Poet*?
- Arthur Miller

Post-Colonialism

Time, Memory, the Past (the Future) and Nostalgia

- Changing Irish society, the Industrial Revolution (late to arrive in Northern Ireland) as represented by the radio and the factory
- The women never marry, so they cannot participate in the future in the typical progenitory way (O'Toole in Harp and Evans, *A Companion to Brian Friel*, p. 181)
- "To be without memory, like Uncle Jack, is perhaps the worst of curses."- Harp & Evans, p. 12 in speaking of *memory as access*
- Harp & Evans, pp. 12-13- *memory is empowering*
- Friel emphasizes that his own memories are "true" because they exist, that "history" is comprised of the way we see it, not "objective truth"
- Simultaneity
- At the time of writing "the problem in Northern Ireland" was approaching at least temporary peace
- Friel is by and large a nationalist

Religion; Women; Dance and the Body

- The African <u>versus</u> the Irish in *Dancing at Lughnasa*
- Uncle (Father) Jack has returned to Ballybeg from missionary work in Africa. While it is never clearly stated in the play, he was sent home.
- This complex character occupies the liminal space between the Celtic, the Catholic, and the African cultures in the play.
- W. B. Yeats stated, "Things fall apart. The centre doesn't hold." Parallels Achebe!

An Exercise in Perspective

"Are We Telling the Same Story?"

In her essay in *Dramaturgy in the American Theater,* Jane Ann Crum talks about the importance of a production dramaturg and director telling the same story.[4] Crum does so through a narrative outlining the creative-collaboration of a student production dramaturg and student director who got to the conclusion of the project only to realize each was telling completely different stories about the same play text. As expected, the project was disjointed in both form and style, with each collaborator dissatisfied with the experience.

Inspired in part by this account and in part by our own run-ins with poor communication, we devised a simple exercise to serve as a checkpoint for avoiding this pitfall when at all possible. Though this can be done solely as a classroom exercise, we have found this type of conversation to be more than useful in our work within the professional theatre.

Instructions

1. Pair up a director and a production dramaturg (or two dramaturgs with one role-playing the director).

2. Using whatever mode of expression is most appropriate and applicable, take five minutes to tell the story of the play text, including the shape the narrative takes. Those who are more visually oriented, they may want to draw out the arc of the play or create a chart or a map that graphs the progression of scenes, images, or themes.

3. Switch partners and roles.

4. Repeat the exercise later in the term (or production process) to make sure that both are still telling the same story of the play.

This modeling exercise can be accomplished even with a class of production dramaturgs who are all working on different written texts. This can also be done by the solo production dramaturg as it is an

---

4   Jane Ann Crum, "Toward a Dramaturgical Sensibility." In *Dramaturgy in American Theater: A Sourcebook.* Ed. Susan Jonas et al. (New York: Harcourt Brace College Publishers, 1997) 70-7.

adaptation of the age-old written précis or short summary of a longer text, which focuses primarily on salient points.

So You Want to be a Production Dramaturg

The following ten proficiencies point toward a foundational sensibility that will carry any production dramaturg, regardless of level, far. These are, of course, in no particular order. Again, just because a production dramaturg might posses the desire to engage others as creative-collaborative colleagues, it does not mean that others will feel the same way towards the production dramaturg. Nevertheless, the suggestions listed below will serve the production dramaturg well when opening a dialogue on the way to committing acts of dramaturgy.

The desire and stamina to invest in a long-term process of thinking theatrically.

1. The desire and fortitude to do research-type tasks such as tracking down scripts, looking up production histories, distilling author biographical information, discerning meanings of words and phrases, and the like.

2. The desire and energy to continuously read scripts and come up with "I see" statements based on engagement and interaction with the text.

3. The desire and staying power to listen more than speak, monitoring conversations so that the production process stays unified and on track.

4. The desire and willingness to work at being a teacher, whether in front of an audience for a preshow lecture or in a production meeting when discussing 19th century Romanticism.

5. The desire and doggedness to sit through casting sessions, rehearsals, and design meetings, taking continuity notes.

6, The desire to and flair for attending to living playwrights and their artistic proclivities.

7. The desire and dexterity to spend hours typing, retyping, and typing yet again.

8. The desire and dedication to a lifelong process of learning and self-enhancement, even if that means picking up a foreign language or other special skill.

9. The desire and determination to create what can be considered unique, vibrant live theatrical performance events.

Chapter Glossary

Actor's Equity Association: Founded in 1913 as a labor union for professional performers and stage managers, the present day industry monitor has over 35,000 members from New York to Los Angeles and all points in between.

Given circumstances: the who, what, when, where, why, how, and to what extent of a given script; the blueprint for the world of the play

IATSE: International Association of Theatre and Stage Employees is the labor union for professional backstage workers other than stage managers.

Letter of Agreement: a document that clearly outlines the relationship between the production dramaturg and a producing agency

Theatrical Metaphor: a central stage image, whether material or immaterial

Primary source information: first-hand accounts of information regarding people or events, usually in the form of letters, speeches, diaries, newspaper articles, oral history interviews, documents, photographs, and sundry artifacts of the time

Secondary source information: material found within a primary source that is generalized, analyzed, synthesized, interpreted, or evaluated for the sake of discussion. Examples might include text books and web sites.

Spine: the main action of the play, usually expressed sentence format

Theme: a broad idea or message inherent to the play text

World of the play: Derived from the given circumstances, this is a set of norms and expectations given by a playwright regarding how characters survive within the text.

Chapter Three

Conceptual Frameworks

This chapter suggests ways in which the production dramaturg might encourage "ways of seeing" the relationship between the written text and the eventual live performance event. This awareness can be helpful when refining a directorial intention, making design choices, or even devising outreach activities. Admittedly, the entire production team strives for unity and coherence, but commonly the production dramaturg emerges as an "objective eye" for continuity, the unique position held as a creative-collaborator. In the long run, detecting or perceiving patterns within the play text—linguistic, aural, visual, or otherwise—can not only push the rehearsal process towards a greater sense of coherence (further discussed in Chapter Four) but also can enhance the resulting live performance event.

Detecting Patterns

By now most if not all of the production team has gone off to work on their own based on the director's initial statements regarding their vision. The production dramaturg has been in contact with the director on a regular basis. Perhaps the production dramaturg has even been able to directly dialogue with members of the production team. Interestingly, discussions with designers often follow a similar sequence to those with directors. The largest difference is that early talks with designers focus much more on an exploration of visual art, signs and symbols, **localized** and **non-localized space**, use of time and place, and the function of each in executing directorial expectations while retaining a sense of artistic freedom. Admittedly, these collaborators are already well-practiced at committing their own acts of dramaturgy.

Nevertheless, the production dramaturg ought to be prepared for pro-duction-specific tasks at this juncture.

In our experience, it is helpful to think of acts of dramaturgy during this phase —wherein the production dramaturg straddles the occu-pational fence between historian/critic and practitioner—in terms of creating and/or recognizing "**conceptual frameworks**" or what might be referred to as "**webs of knowledge**" or "**informational webs**." By these we mean a group of approaches or "ways of seeing" into a given play text, whether theory-driven or not. We speak in terms of webs or groups for a couple of reasons. First, we desire to debunk monolithic script analyses that focus on a single "theme" and imply there is one "right answer" to the "seeing" process. Second, we find that it is often at a juncture where two or more ideas converge that we find in our own work some powerful fuel for a unifying path to a **production conceit**.

For example, after preliminary design meetings for *On the Verge*, the set designer and production dramaturg continued to dialogue via e-mail as each searched for an inspirational image to express how time and place, fantasy and language are manipulated by the Overmyer. Eventually both were drawn to a particular line in the script referenc-ing a kaleidoscope. In another instance as the director for *Dancing at Lughnasa* sought ways to remind spectators of Ireland's tempestu-ous history, the production dramaturg offered the set designer several images of protests, flags and graffiti. Sometimes designers contact the production dramaturg with specific questions and research agendas, as was the case when the props designer for *Richard III* needed dimen-sions and shapes for early 20th century toy (wooden) blocks. Though many of these conversations start during the pre-production phase, dialogue about specific research-oriented questions from designers may well continue well into the production's build phase.

As mentioned, the production dramaturg's focused energy and pragmatic responsibilities overlap throughout the creative-collaborative process. Reading the play text again and again during the pre-produc-tion phase with an eye for emergent patterns is no exception. Drawing on information already gathered, this part of the production drama-turg's job concentrates on noticing relationships across time and history,

Img. 3.1 *Dancing at Lughnasa*. McLeod Theatre. Dir.: OleSegun Ojewuyi. Photo: Robert Holcombe. Notice the celtic monolith and armband. Both were inspired by dramaturgical research and discussions with the director.

posing focused questions about those relationships and keeping the pre-production artistic conversation going when it gets bogged down. The fledgling production dramaturg, as previously noted, time and again executes the "hunting and gathering" phase with great aplomb and vigor. The "devil"—or at least danger—is in distilling the details. As such, a production dramaturg must take great care to never "lose sight of the forest for the trees" when seeking out emergent patterns. Interestingly, these seemingly benign patterns might, in fact, be traces of an intentional or unintentional **organizing principle** on the playwright or creator's part. These may also inform a director of moments to **bracket** in the live performance.

With experience and continued reading, a production dramaturg will perpetually improve the ability to make connections and comparisons across history, time, cultures, literary genres, and the like. We offer the following chart as an example of a way to accelerate and sustain this growth. Initially created to help student production dramaturgs compare plays from across history, the chart is purposefully broad in scope. The idea here is not to create a "one size fits all" approach to searching for patterns, but rather to suggest that the production dramaturg may devise a chart to serve as a check list for any number of factors that emerge from a given written text. Obviously, a check list or chart is by no means a "dramaturgical Holy Grail" because it allows no space for explanatory notes or equivocation. The chart may sometimes seem rather arbitrary, but its completion provides one way of seeing that provides the production dramaturg with a spring board for further investigation.

	Our Town	*Dancing at Lughnasa*	*Titus Andronicus*	*The Crucible*
Myth			X	
Ritual	X	X		X
History		X	X	X
Non-localized space	X	X	X	
Presentational	X	X	X	
Representational				X
Heightened language			X	X
Chorus				X
Conventions	X	X	X	
Emphasis on gender	X	X	X	X
Masks/Costume				X
Spirituality/ Religion	X	X	X	X
Audience participates				

Notice for example the multiple categories that apply to *The Crucible*. Interestingly, both playwright Arthur Miller and critic/theatre historian Brenda Murphy use the word "ritual" in their discussions of the play text. Not only does *The Crucible* tell the tale of the Salem

Witch Trials but also its rituals of accusation evoke the processes by which Miller was questioned when he appeared before the House Un-American Activities Committee. Fittingly, Miller's stage directions for *The Crucible* are evocative of this experience. We should note that since the use of a chart or checklist is intended for pre-production preparation, the production dramaturg does not employ categories that consider ways in which a director and designers might depart from the written text in the creation of their visual design. If nothing else, then, a production dramaturg may draft such a chart as a "litmus test" for whether a play will fit into a season that is being organized thematically. Perhaps a more effective visual representation of how thematic concerns or theoretical perspectives converge in viewing a given text might be to construct a "Venn Diagram" (see Fig. 3.1).

Sometimes a director carries theory into production without prompting from the production dramaturg. Just as with information on production history, it is the director's call as to how much theory to share with performers. In the case of St. Louis Black Repertoire Theatre-Southern Illinois University Carbondale Theatre joint production of *Death and the King's Horseman*, the production dramaturgs read voraciously about both the play and playwright as well as about Yoruba cosmology, mythology, crafts and social structure—specifically addressing the marketplace not only as the locus of economic transactions, a bustling site filled with the thrill of buying and exchange, but also as a place where destinies are exchanged. The director, a Nigerian living in the United States, was already familiar with many of the concepts that were new to the dramaturgical team. The task of the dramaturgy team, then, at the director's urging, became one of selecting appropriate resource material to assist the director in conveying a non-Western ideology and performance approach to a Western cast. The resulting production resource pack did so by concentrating on notions expressed by Soyinka's author note at the beginning of every published version of the play. In addition to the glossary and expected material, the resource pack included a section entitled "Connecting Concepts to Production" that incorporated working definitions of "ritual", "transition", "transformation" and "liminal space." Another section drew comparisons and contrasts to famous Western plays. "Space" was addressed as a place of struggle, contested and non-localized. All of this was presented to the performers during the first rehearsal.

Ultimately, finding possible lenses through which to view a text can come quickly and easily with director and production dramaturg moving readily along to a production concept, or the arrival at an approach can be painstakingly slow. Consequently, this stage of preparation is an exercise in connectivity, selection, and, most importantly, persistence.

Ways of Seeing with Theory

Identifiable patterns can lead to **theoretical frameworks** which, in turn, can lead to enticing production options for a director during early planning discussions and subsequent production meetings. The problem is that theory in the production process has gotten a bad name. This is due, in large part, to the perception that many practitioners often have, regarding theory and performance practices as two separate endeavors that rarely, if ever, converge. We disagree. In fact, the *Oxford English Dictionary* indicates that the Greek *thea*—common to both theatre (*theatron*, or seeing place) and theory—indicates a way of looking at or speculating about a group of findings. Thus theory, much like theatre, is a way of seeing.

Obviously it is wise for the production dramaturg to heed the old adage about "knowing your spectatorship" when attempting to advocate an appropriate theoretical framework. In practice a production dramaturg interfaces with *several* audiences—the director, designers and other members of the production team, performers, publicists, teachers, learners, spectators, and the like—which immediately complicates the situation. The primary concern of the production dramaturg, then, is figuring out how to appropriately express the nature and efficacy of theory in direct application to both the written text and the eventual live performance event in a way that engages all interested parties. Crucial to this act of dramaturgy are notions of degree and tone. That is, to what degree is it necessary to *name* a particular theoretical approach as long as the production dramaturg captures its essence and applicability? Of what use is it for the production dramaturg to spout off theoretical terminology and constructs if it means putting forth a pedantic and condescending tone?

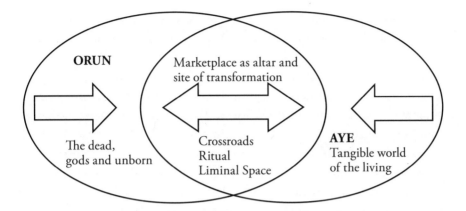

Fig. 3.1 Based on the Yoruban proverb, "The world (aye) is a marketplace we visit, the otherworld (orun) is home" (Aye Loja Orun Nile), this Venn diagram for *Death and the King's Horseman* represents how Soyinka's play captures a fictive world in transition between that of the dead, the gods and the unborn and the tangible world of the living. In Yoruba cosmology these worlds are always interrelated. This information influenced multiple design elements.

We find that theoretical frameworks can often be incorporated into talking points and introduced into dialogue with the director, designers, and other collaborators without being too self-conscious. This early connection-making leads to possible webs of information or conceptual sets, and even to critical theory as it might be applied to the production. In the case of Post-colonialism and the *Dancing at Lughnasa* talking points example in Chapter Two, both the director and production dramaturg explored several ideas that concentrated on African/Celtic/Catholic connections, ritual, and notions of time/memory/history (timelines). From this emerged a theory-driven conceptual framework, which drove the visual design for the live performance. Most notable among designer choices were the ever-present "monolith" (a Celtic-inspired memorial stone), the political armband worn by the narrator Michael (an emblem of Irish political strife for decades), and a sound design that blended African drum rhythms and traditional Irish tunes (see Img. 3.1).

Another way to convey possible theory-driven ways of seeing the written text is to jot down a couple of paragraphs describing what emerges from your close reading of the script. At an early meeting, the production dramaturg for *On the Verge* brought tidbits of information to the table. These were a few carefully positioned comments regarding how Overmyer, through the anti-Aristotelian manipulation of time, place and action, offers a humorous social commentary on American hubris, expansion and colonialism. The production dramaturg shared these with the director in prose form. The director ultimately focused more on the three separate and distinct journeys of the women than on explicit strains of feminist criticism: the geographical journey, the journey of the women learning about each other, and the inner journey that each must take by herself. Manifestations of these journeys—both inner and outer—found their way into the visual design. In this case, a theory-driven way of seeing led to an embedded exploration of feminist ideals in the live production. This type of "tidbit" prose, regardless of the play text, can and usually does grow out of the "Letter to the Director" model. In a number of circumstances, this sort of write-up is the crux of that entire communiqué.

Theory-driven "Tidbits" excerpted from *On the Verge, or The Geography of Yearning*

Southern Illinois University Carbondale
Anne Fletcher, Lead Production Dramaturg
Lori Merrill-Fink, Director

19th century Female Travelers and *On the Verge*

While Eric Overmyer insists that the characters in *On the Verge* are not directly based on any "real life" women, he admits to having been inspired by 19th century female travel writing. The character names neatly coincide with those of three female explorers—the American <u>Fanny</u> Bullock Workman (1859-1925); British <u>Mary</u> Kingsley (1862-1900), and French-born <u>Alexandra</u> David-Neel (1868-1969). In fact, Overmyer utilizes journal writing as his technique to comment on and separate the short vignettes that compose his play. Moreover, some of the incidents he portrays (for example the joke about eating and drinking with cannibals) come straight from Mary Kingsley's travelogue.

Feminist critiques have revealed the levels to which female travelers have been subjected to much stereotyping by the dominant paradigm. By and large they have been viewed as oddities, eccentrics somehow divorced from the realities of their worlds. While their bravery and tenacity have been acknowledged, their writing itself has been considered precious and non-literary and the veracity of their statements has been questioned.

These female explorers "went against the grain" of the Victorian world in which they lived, a male-dominated world where they could not buy property without the consent of husbands or fathers—a male-dominated world of domesticity for most middle-class women, one in which a "woman's place" was in the private sphere. And, much has been written about the physical restrictions applied to the woman's body of the time—the ubiquitous corset.

The 19th century, of course, represents a world fraught with colonialism, and the status of these women travelers and writers was problematic, caught between the conflicting demands of the discourse of feminism and that of implicit imperialism. So, to view the female traveler/writer as simply an individual "bucking the norm" ignores facets of her experience and of her narrative of her own experience. *On the Verge*, of course, is not docudrama, but Overmyer's three female travelers challenge customary modes of behaviors in curious, amusing and timeless ways.

To See or Not to See

It goes without saying that the best way for a production dramaturg to enhance their facility with theory and criticism is sustained practice. Within a learning environment this is easily done through assigned readings from a theory/criticism text coupled with an instructor-led review of critical concepts that takes advantage of small group discussion/activity techniques. We find that revisiting and rereading the most recent editions of Janelle Reinelt and Joseph Roach's *Critical Theory and Performance* and Mark Fortier's *Theatre/Theory* as well as *Theatre Topics*, *Theatre Research International* and *Text and Performance Quarterly* are easy ways to stay abreast of current convergences of theory and praxis.

As an exercise that resembles the daily practice of a production dramaturg we ask our learners to select a text and then "check in with" that text *vis-à-vis* a list of potential theoretical approaches, perhaps by listing the page numbers from the text where each theory-driven way of seeing might be of use. In this way the applicability of a given theoretical framework can be tested in a quantifiable manner. If there are only a couple of instances of queer theory in *Our Town*, for example, then how effective might it be to foreground that in production? If there are numerous possibilities for applying feminist criticism to *The Taming of the Shrew*, then might not a director want to "go there"? Then again, too many theory-driven ways of seeing a written text point to the *over-use* of or *over*-reliance on critical theory by the production dramaturg. This often indicates that the production dramaturg needs to turn away from theory as a way of seeing. In fact, some of the most interesting moments in our own work are when we realize that a theoretical framework is a proverbial dead end for the live production and that we must embrace another way of seeing.

	Our Town	*Dancing at Lughnasa*	*Titus Andronicus*	*The Crucible*
Semiotics	X			
Phenomenology	X	X		
Post-Structuralism				
Psychoanalytic Theory	X	X	X	X
Deconstruction			X	
Feminist(s) Criticism	X	X	X	X
Post-Colonialism		X	X	X
Gender	X	X	X	X
Queer Theory	X		X	

Ways of Seeing without Theory

It is important to realize that not every play text or live performance calls for a theoretical framework. In fact, forcing a theory-driven frame onto a play text and its performance is detrimental if not disastrous. Frequently there are exciting ways see into a play text without the use

Img. 3.2 *The Complete Works of William Shakespeare (abridged)*. Illinois Shakespeare Festival. Dir.: Bill Jenkins. Photo: R. Lee Kennedy. Beer, boots and bluegrass have arrived.

of critical theory. For example, director Bill Jenkins' *The Complete Works of William Shakespeare (abridged)* wove a "NASCAR experience" throughout, layering in a healthy dose of beer, Bluegrass and boots. The production concept worked well in performance, and was never overly burdened with theory as the production team worked to realize it on stage. Once in rehearsals the production dramaturg spent a lot of time and attention in close consultation with the director, focusing on the moment-to-moment maintenance of the conceit just as would have been done if a theoretical framework were the chosen gauge of continuity.

Every so often it is a non-theory driven perspective that leads the production dramaturg to see emergent patterns that somehow relate to a theoretical framework. Some of the common places we begin this process include:

- Period and Styles
- Genre-specific conventions
- Language-driven; Character-Driven; Spectacle-Driven; etc.
- Memory Play and links to dream interpretation
- Silences, Rhythm and Tempo
- Interdisciplinary lens that borrows from such places as visual art [Surrealism], music, science [String Theory], business, etcetera
- Historical Personages/Historification
- Time-lines
- External popular culture references

What is most important is that the production dramaturg clearly articulate both what is known and what is seen in ways that benefit the pre-production process.

For example, the plays of Suzan-Lori Parks present special difficulties as she has devised a particular structural and auditory plan. Occasionally Parks shares parts of this plan in some sort of prefatory remarks. Sometimes she does not. Some of our student production dramaturgs are initially bewildered when asked to look for patterns in her early pieces. Once they discover that the dramaturgical "meat" lay in the spaces, holes, and interstices (either expressed in Parks' phrasing or what was left unsaid), they warm to the task. Similarly, the production dramaturg for a university production of *A Raisin in the Sun* returns to the play text in search of patterns, discovering an important one related to money transactions. The production dramaturg notes at least eight instances where money literally switched hands. Calling the pattern "Walter Lee: Show Me the Money" the production dramaturg uses it as a way of seeing, graphing the action of the play with regard to Walter Lee (see Fig. 3.2).

Moving a period piece from one era to another is a complex enterprise. This process often requires that the production dramaturg adopt a non-theory-driven perspective while still attending to continuity. Clear directorial decisions must be made regarding substitutions of items from one era with those of another era, especially with costume pieces,

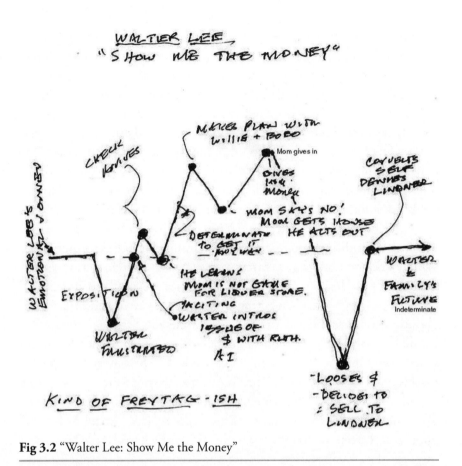

Fig 3.2 "Walter Lee: Show Me the Money"

props and music. A great example of these substitutions appeared in director Kristin Horton's noire-like *Richard III* at the Riverside Theatre Shakespeare Festival. Period rifles, bayonets, pistols and helmets, for example, stood in for swords, lances, daggers, and face shields. All the same, the production dramaturg must also realize that some replacements can become self-conscious and draw unwarranted attention when there is an apparent disconnect between the words the characters speak and the items to which they refer. An example might be the addition of a laptop, a cell phone or a can of SPAM to an otherwise Elizabethan-looking *The Taming of the Shrew* in order to "update" it without considering how the entire visual design needs adjustment in order to make the modernizations sensible within the world of the play in performance.

Given the special considerations that come with working on a translation/adaptation or a musical, the production dramaturg should consider turning to a non-theory way of seeing as a starting point. In the case of Lexington Children Theatre's production of *A Christmas Carol*, director J. Russell Couch was concerned with developing not only a fresh one hour adaptation but also a stimulating visual design. After a few conversations, the production dramaturg set about reading and watching several theatre, television and film versions of the classic tale. Though this did not yield a particular way of seeing, it did afford the production dramaturg an opportunity to find less commonly used lines and portions of scenes, integrating them into the adaptation. It was not until director and production dramaturg talked about issues of time and memory that a framework surfaced wherein period-specific elements of Western theatre history would serve as the conceptual framework. Six performers acting much like the Greek Chorus would play all secondary roles, with the seventh solely as Scrooge. The setting would have suggestive elements but take full advantage of non-localized space. The Ghost of Christmas Past would be the Chorus in neutral mask(s) chanting in unison. The Ghost of Christmas Present became a fusion of Victorian and 20th century US conceptions of Santa Claus. The Ghost of Christmas Future turned into a large "Angel of Death" puppet on casters with a manipulator inside the base. This way of seeing was doubly appealing because the Kentucky Education Reform Act required learners of all ages be exposed to fundamental concepts and principles of the arts and humanities, which this approach would clearly encompass.

An hour and a half down the road, Actors Theatre of Louisville presents *A Christmas Carol* as well. In fact, it is the second longest running version in the US. The challenge at Actors is keeping the live performance event fresh and exciting year after year, while recognizing the production remains a holiday tradition for generations of patrons. Over the last five years, the same production dramaturg has worked with three different directors. Each director has had their own ideas, and every year each has wanted to change any number of things, from adding more songs to changing the way the phantoms and Marley are portrayed on stage. The production dramaturg's role has been important on this production—being obsessively familiar with both the Dickens story and adapted play text—in helping the directors come up with cohesive new ideas in order to improve on an already great show; making sure to stay in touch with the adaptor (Barbara Field) to make sure she approves of any changes they are thinking of making; distributing those changes to the production team and cast as well as, perhaps most importantly, making sure that the new ideas honor Dickens' story. All of this is in hopes of keeping the Actors' spectatorship as entertained and enthralled with the ghostly tale as they have been for over thirty years. This show is often the first that children from the area see, and it is not uncommon to notice multiple generations of a family enjoying it together. Given this, the production dramaturg monitors changes so as to avoid alienating returning spectators while keeping each staging fresh. Admittedly, this is a fine line to walk. Ultimately, large theatres like the Guthrie, the Alley, Theatre Calgary, and so many more rely on *A Christmas Carol* to be one of the biggest family show year after year, not only for the financial rewards it brings to the theatre but also for the good will it generates in the community—the region—which the theatre serves. This provides interesting challenges for a production dramaturg. Dickens surely would have loved that his tale has made such a contribution to the English speaking theatres (although we do imagine he would have been upset that his copyright has expired).

The following questions are helpful in testing a production conceit for overall continuity. These may also be used when making decisions concerning period pieces and adaptations of classic narratives such as *A Christmas Carol*. More times than not a blended, multi-period production can be more successful than one in which minute details are transported across history and time.

Action

Does the conceit complement the given beginning, middle and end of the text?

Does the conceit hold up as the text in production moves from one event to the next?

Does the conceit cloud or clarify the overall story of the action of the play?

Auditory cues

Does the conceit allow aural moments (music or otherwise) to naturally emerge?

Doe the conceit permit aural choices that contribute to the meaning of the play in performance in a meaningful way?

Does the conceit use aural choices to create mood and atmosphere that coordinate with the larger message of the play?

Intrinsic Meaning

Does the conceit reveal or bury the essential story of the play?

Does the conceit expose or veil the givens of the play text?

Does the conceit open up or close off ways of seeing the story of the play in production?

Language

Does the conceit match the exposition and spoken décor of the play text?

Does the conceit warrant the removal, adaptation or addition of words or lines?

Does the conceit allow for the message of the story to emerge in performance?

Performers

Does the conceit allow for vocal and physical qualities to match the givens of the play text?

Does the conceit allow the performers to clearly differentiate one role from one another in performance?

Does the conceit allow performers latitude in the building of their character?

Spectacle

Does the conceit permit scenery and props to reveal time and place?

Does the conceit allow costumes to reveal personality as well as historical era and the like?

Does the conceit provide for lighting, special effects and projections to direct attention appropriately?

Many regional theatres, including Actors Theatre of Louisville, The American Repertory Theatre in Cambridge, Massachusetts and Centaur Theatre in Montreal, have as part of their mission to both re-imagine and re-envision the classics. Often, live performances at these venues only suggest a period, intentionally mixing eras to create a hybrid style. Regardless of the situation, monolithic (or even partial) period moves must be carefully deliberated and continually monitored in rehearsals through the use of "I see" statements and questions.

So You Want to be a Production Dramaturg

As noted in the Introduction, a number of dramaturgical acts at this stage of the process are conducted concurrently with other procedures and tasks outlined in Chapters One and Two. Some of the **skill sets** a production dramaturg develops over time are equally applicable to pre-production solo work, in preliminary work with a director, and in fact stretch across the entire production (and post-production) process. Consider various tasks described earlier, like "Talking Points", "Letter to the Director", and even the Glossary of Terms and Concepts. The production dramaturg's notebook, like the evolving production itself, is a work in progress. In order for the production dramaturg's research to be helpful to director, performers and designers alike as well as efficacious to the overall live performance event, work completed early on must be revisited, adapted, expanded, focused, and perhaps even discarded. It is a good idea, then, to return to information within "Talking Points" or the "Letter to the Director" periodically throughout the production process. Thinking of dramaturgical acts as ongoing conversations rather than as lone research activities helps in understanding the crucial move from "hunting and gathering" to interpreting and contributing in significant ways. We discuss the complexities of this transition further in the next section.

Chapter Glossary

Bracket: to set off or highlight in some way, as with a moment in a scene or particular sorts of moments throughout a performance.

Conceptual framework(s): the utilization of various lenses or windows to view a text; more than one theoretical approach used in combination, for example Feminism and Post-colonialism.

Informational webs: a group of approaches or "ways of seeing" into a given play text, whether theory-driven or not.

Localized space: theatrical space indicated by the written text and/ or production elements that provides specific location(s) such as a living room

Non-localized space: theatrical space that appears physically or architecturally neutral but may become a variety of locations through its use; often related to imagery or "word painting" as we frequently learn location from the characters' lines.

Organizing principle: a method of focusing on certain aspects of a written text; not necessarily theory driven, but rather emanating from a [re]examination of the text itself; the process of deriving an organizing principle might involve counting the number of times a particular image recurs, for example.

Production conceit: the manifestation of final design choices as integrated with the live bodies of performers on stage that grows out of the directorial concept; a realized approach to a play text and the tangible articulation of the directorial concept in live performance

Skill sets: abilities and/or methodologies acquired that are beneficial in viewing both text and performance; may be critical, theoretical or practical.

Theoretical frameworks: approaches or lenses through which to view a text (and production) drawn from literary/dramatic theory and criticism or from strategies of analysis from other disciplines (i.e. String Theory). For example, the "scientific method" might be applicable to Naturalism.

Web(s) of knowledge: also referred to as "informational webs," a group of approaches or "ways of seeing" into a given play text, whether theory-driven or not. Knowledge drawn from more than one discipline might converge, thus the notion of a "web."

PART TWO
Rehearsals

This second segment of the book seeks both to illustrate and to explicate an array of responsibilities that a production dramaturg might have during a rehearsal process. Given that every live theatrical event calls for a unique approach to both preparation and execution, each rehearsal process will be different as well. The fluctuations a production dramaturg experiences from one process to another not only involve an adjustment in the kinds of pragmatic tasks completed but also a shift in the way a production dramaturg sees themselves within the creative-collaborative environment fostered by the director. The ideas we present in this section naturally grow out of the material presented in Section One. At times we return to material introduced in the previous section in order to highlight ways in which solid preparation is foundational to a positive, productive experience not only for the production dramaturg but also for performers, director and technical staff. Given our diverse experiences both within the professional and college/university settings, this section of *The Process of Dramaturgy* provides best practices common to our work regardless of venue.

Chapter Four will address a variety of ways in which the basics of Section One might be put into practice while in rehearsal, and Chapter Five attends to what it means to be a production dramaturg while working on a new play in development.

Chapter Four

An Eye for Continuity

This chapter contends that even as the function of the production dramaturg is modified depending on the nature of the director's vision for creative-collaboration, there are a variety of stable points of reference from which to initiate effective and influential rehearsal work. As anyone interested in acts of dramaturgy might expect, a few of the tasks described within this chapter may well be completed along with the preparation work outlined in Section One. In any case, there are specific functions in which a production dramaturg cannot engage until performers, design assistants and shop staff(s) are brought into the process—such as table work, production meetings, run-throughs, and outreach ideas. What we most clearly mark within this chapter, then, are intermittent movements away from the solitary nature of generating production resource materials and suggesting a frame from which to examine the play towards the shared undertaking of staging a live performance event and double-checking choices in the name of consistent storytelling in all areas of the production.

Preparing and Editing the Written Text

As we mentioned earlier, the production dramaturg often embarks on preparatory processes much earlier than other members of the artistic team. When working on a classic text such as those of Euripides, Shakespeare, Moliere or even a modern classic Federal Theatre Project play, one of the most important contributions a production dramaturg can make to the live performance event is preparing and editing the play text. This holds true as well for those projects that call for a translation to be made. When done in close consultation with the director, the preparation and editing of this document can go a long way toward providing an exciting threshold from which to launch rehearsals, which will undoubtedly lead to a stimulating production for performer, designer, technician, and spectator alike.

Though being integrated into the process at the earliest planning stages is admittedly not practical in all situations, the production dramaturg excluded from preparing and editing the written text is grossly underutilized. That is, since issues of words, themes, metaphor, rhythm, context (both within and without of the world of the play) and the like are being dealt with on a line by line basis, who better to have involved in this process than the production dramaturg, armed with the information outlined in Chapter One? For our purposes here, we are presuming that the director (or artistic director) has chosen the public domain text to be used as a starting point. Naturally, if provided the opportunity, this is another area where the production dramaturg will be of great use because of a specialized knowledge of particular translators, adaptors or yet-to-be-revived manuscripts hiding in special collections at an academic institution or library.

With the preliminary version of the text in hand, the first thing that a production dramaturg must realize is that there is absolutely nothing sacred about a given classic text. These are documents generated by writers during a situated time in history and are therefore products of that situated time, often riddled with obscure references, phrases and anachronisms not readily accessible to most contemporary theatre patrons. These dramatic texts are also quite lengthy when considering the average attention span of a contemporary society reared on Blackberry communication, on-demand programming and the ability to digitally record television while excluding commercials. Lastly, the writers of these texts themselves often borrowed profusely from existing material when preparing and editing the work for performance in order to fit the prevailing interests of their own time, place and spectatorship. At this point, some may wish to vociferously object to the notion that the work of Shakespeare, for example, is not sacred to the Western literary tradition. Remember, though, that a production dramaturg is much more interested in the play-in-performance, which calls for much different sensibilities than the play-as-literature. In fact, between Quarto One,

Quarto Two and the First Folio there are so many editorial and print-erly revisions of Shakespeare's plays that producing one as it sounded in The Rose or The Globe is quite improbable. However, a literary analysis of changes from one edition to another can prove useful in rehearsal when revising the prepared text to be used in performance.

Keeping issues of storytelling and arc at the fore, the production dramaturg must next read the text with three things in mind: *time*, *tension* and *tone*. In this case, time refers to the prescribed preferences of the theatre and its spectatorship. For example, returning patrons of the Illinois Shakespeare Festival have come to expect a first act that is somewhere around fifty-five minutes and a second act of forty-five to fifty-five minutes, with a fifteen minute intermission separating the acts. Given this, the production dramaturg must try to prepare a writ-ten text that mirrors these expectations. While we hesitate whenever art is viewed as a quantifiable entity, running time is a reality of the production process. As such, there are ways in which it can and should be approached from an almost mathematical standpoint. In light of this, there is a basic formula that works well when attempting to gauge the overall reading time of the written text:

Total Number of Lines x 3 seconds for performer
delivery / 60 = Reading Time

Time in production will vary from this reading time as performer busi-ness, sound and lights, as well as special effects, are layered in to the **performance text**. Oftentimes this layering will result in a longer time and thus call for more editing of the spoken text while at other times this layering will provide a sense of momentum, driving the spoken text at a much quicker pace. It is also during the text preparation phase that discussions about whether or not to take an intermission often begin. All of this said, we need to make it quite clear that preparing and editing a play text for time is the *least important* element in the text preparation process. Keep in mind that many a dubious act of drama-turgy has been committed in the name of making time. In fact, text preparation is rarely as easy as cutting for time.

For example, when Actors Theatre of Louisville staged *The Tempest* the director was most interested in focusing on the father/daughter story, so the production dramaturg and director rearranged and cut to focus storytelling on the Prospero/Miranda relationship. In doing so, Act Four and Act Five were reorganized so that the masque emerged as a wedding at the end of the performance, giving Prospero the opportunity to give Miranda away. The entire text was also re-punctuated after consulting several published versions including the Folio. The director for the aforementioned production of *Richard III* wanted to focus the story of the play on Richard's moral ambiguity and (albeit questionable) sexual motivation for domination, creating an almost *film noire*-like world. The production dramaturg worked with the director, assistant director and the performer playing Richard not only to re-punctuate the text—after consulting the Arden version, the Folio and the Folger version—but also to remove material not vital to that storyline. This process was initiated months *before* rehearsals and continued until opening night. As these examples indicate, both tension and tone (and themes) are much more important issues to attend to in the text preparation process because they work to activate language while focusing on the performative strengths of a given text. Tension and tone are consistently shaped by considering the contextual intent of each line within the bounds of a director's concept.

Tension refers to the dramatic conflict of the written text, or what drives the play from beginning to end. Closely related is tone, or how that conflict is communicated through stage directions, dialogue and character interactions. In deriving an understanding of each, the production dramaturg needs to listen carefully to the director's ideas as to what the core of the story is exactly. This is often gleaned from the first few conversations with the director and may reveal itself as an image, word or phrase from the play itself that is continually referenced. It might emerge as an overarching theme the director finds buried within the dialogue, or grow out of a political leaning the director carries with them in daily life. Whatever the case, it is a fruitless endeavor to push ahead without listening to what the director has already clued into in preparing. This is not to suggest that presenting other ideas to the director is uncalled for or inappropriate. We find that acting as devil's advocate or as sounding board is the best way to proceed. Given this information, the production dramaturg engages in text preparation knowing what will not or cannot be edited out of the text—whether an entire scene or an arcane word. In the end the goal is to prepare a written text that avoids what director Catherine Weidner refers to as the "Hey Agnes" moment in production. This is the point in the live performance event when a patron leans over to "Agnes" and says: "Hey Agnes, what does that word mean?" or "Hey Agnes, did you understand that?" In this instant the patrons are no longer engaged by the story being told on stage, due to uncertainty if not complete misunderstanding. They have been "taken out" of the live performance.

In all steps along the preparation and editing process it is best to consult at least three different versions of the play in question. It may even prove useful to listen to film versions to get a sense of the rhythm used when translating the play text into a screenplay. These versions may also be what are most familiar to some patrons, so having knowledge of them also allows the director to take into account, to some extent, what has already been seen by some of the anticipated spectatorship. Many of the same concerns must be attended to when preparing an adaptation or re-envisioning an updated version of a well-known text, such as the previously mentioned *A Christmas Carol*.

Planning and Production Meetings

As a member of the artistic team primarily concerned with overall continuity, the production dramaturg must focus time and energy both in early planning meetings and in production meetings to listening to and taking note of terms and concepts being bandied about, with special attention to the production concept as it evolves. In this capacity, the production dramaturg is uniquely positioned to facilitate cross-fertilization within the artistic team, leading to a stronger sense of unity in the final live performance event. These meetings are also venues in which the production dramaturg ought to be aware of where people are heading in terms of their own artistic interpretation of the directorial intention and "feed" that energy. Sometimes this entails private conversations with a director regarding choices—design or otherwise—that seemingly run counter to the written text. At others, this means sharing images, music or further research to bolster a choice. At still other times, this might mean asking a clarifying question near the end of a production meeting. Whether involved in the planning

process from the beginning or not, one of the most important functions of the production dramaturg in these types of meetings is the
tracking of vocabulary used when talking about the work at hand.

An example of the need for the production dramaturg to function in this capacity comes from a recent university production of a
MFA thesis play. In this case there were some presumptions made by
both writer and director regarding terminology foundational to the
production design. The ambiguous use of jargon ultimately resulted
in rather substantial problems for the final scenic design. Within the
stage directions the playwright describes a non-illusionistic setting in
which characters wander through what was identified as the "collective
conscious"—an apparent appropriation of Jungian psychology lingo.
The description goes on to call for characters to be bombarded by archetypes—again a loaded term that was not clearly defined within the
stage direction. No one at the early production meetings, including the
production dramaturg, stopped long enough to ask for clarification from
the writer. Eventually the director and scenic designer agreed to move
forward with elements of archetype, abandoning Jungian examples in
favor of those that might read clearer to a contemporary spectatorship.
Designer and director both struggled to come to a consensus as to what
an archetype would look like within the visual design. This struggle led
to delays and resulted in a final rush to put something on stage. What
eventually materialized was a random selection of archetypal imagery
that added little to the production design. Months later as the designer
wrote of this process in a thesis, the production dramaturg realized that
what the director (and writer) was looking for were *icons* (markers of
certain ideals and concepts) and not *archetypes* (a pervasive idea, image,
or symbol that forms part of the collective unconscious). Had someone
caught this miscommunication at an early design or production meeting, then valuable time at technical rehearsals could have been saved.
More importantly, a more unified production would have most defi-
nitely emerged. In our experiences within academic theatre specifically,
the production dramaturg most likely possesses the critical vocabulary
necessary to notice this kind of occurrence as sometimes overly exuber-
ant directors and designers talk at cross-purposes and THINK they are
meaning the seem thing. This is not to suggest similar occurrences do

not happen in professional theatre. If they do, however, then they are atypical.

The type of miscommunication, lack of communication or lack of agreement on the uses of terminology referenced above can plague a production, infecting all aspects of continuity. Often these related problems emanate NOT from somewhat obscure references (like those of Jungian psychology) but even from the most basic theatrical terms, like "Realism" or "surreal." The production dramaturg needs to engage in a **formal analysis** of the text at hand, *beginning* with the written text as opposed to outside sources of interest. This type of analysis (at face value simplistic) prepares a production dramaturg for active participation in fruitful discussions of form, structure, genre, and style of production with the members of the artistic staff. Thorough and advanced preparation allows the production dramaturg as creative-collaborator to honestly pose text-based questions like "What do you mean by…" and "Can you give me an example of…" in the name of continuity. Continuity in form and style can be assured only when it is clear that everyone at the table is telling the same story through the same means.

It is just as important for the production dramaturg to be at ease with the deployment of traditional theatrical vocabulary regarding late 19th century/early 20th century theatrical "**-isms**" that were initiated as a response to artistic movements such as Naturalism and Representational Realism. These terms are used with notorious inconsistency both in theory and in practice. Knowing this—and knowing the problems of terminology usage in critical theory and **post-modernism**—the production dramaturg can proceed with eyes and ears open, willing to continually ask for clarification. Most script analysis and introduction to the theatre texts offer glossaries that include at least rudimentary definitions for these theatrical forms and styles (See Appendix A).

Generating Production Resource Packs

In creating a production resource pack from the materials discussed in Chapter One, the production dramaturg should always emphasize information that will be of most use to performers as each goes about preparing to build their characters. Because these packs are distributed early in rehearsals it is important to provide only information and images that further describe the given circumstances of the play. Once in rehearsal there will undoubtedly be requests for more specific information, but it is important that the entire company receive the same basic pack of information. Usually this basic pack includes short write-ups that inform the overall creation of the world of the play in production. Of course the contents of the production resource pack will not only vary depending on the chosen script but also on the experience level of cast members. That is, the types of information provided to a cast of undergraduate students staging *Titus Andronicus* will be quite different from that given to a cast of professional Shakespeare performers. If the company is a mix of both professionals and amateurs, as was the case with *Death and the King's Horseman*, then a midpoint in both tone and content must be found. In all cases, there are a few important questions the production dramaturg must ask when putting together the production resource pack:

- What references, obscure or otherwise, to published texts, geographic locations, or cultural customs might need clarification?
- What element of the conceptual framework needs to be reinforced, highlighted or brought to the forefront of a performer's process?
- What images best help illustrate the world of the play as decided by the director?
- To what extent are playwright biography, production history, and socio-cultural influences vital to the preparation of performers?

In select instances it may prove helpful to develop a specific pack of information for each character. For example, the director of *Dancing at Lughnasa* modeled character motivations and costume design choices for the narrator Michael after Irish revolutionary leader Michael Collins. The production dramaturg supplied the performer with a folder of information regarding Collins' life and times to aid in rehearsal work and character preparation.

Table of Contents from *Titus Andronicus* Resource Pack
Illinois Shakespeare Festival
Scott R. Irelan, Production Dramaturg
Catherine Weidner, Director

Table of Contents

Read Through

Nearly all of the productions we work on, regardless of venue, open with a small number of rehearsal sessions devoted to the sharing of information by the artistic and production staff. This may be the first and only time until technical rehearsals that everyone, performers included, will be in the same place at the same time. Usually the first order of business is the presentation of ideas by the director and the designers. Of late, it has become common for the production dramaturg to be called upon to share some relevant findings not included in the production resource pack. Since time is a precious commodity, the production dramaturg needs to be succinct and focused. We tend to keep these three things in mind as we organize our thoughts:

- Keep within a 10-15 minute time span unless otherwise directed.
- Clear all remarks and information with the director prior.
- Include images, moving or otherwise, and link them with what the designers have used as inspiration if at all possible

This is not a time to introduce divergent or tangential ideas. Rather, the work of the production dramaturg at the first read-through is to point up issues of continuity and offer support to the director's conceptual framework.

In the case of the Illinois Shakespeare Festival's first rehearsal of *The Taming of the Shrew,* the production dramaturg concentrated on the geography of Northern Italy and how long it would take to travel between each city by horse (see next page). With a large map of Italy (which had been cross-referenced with a period map) mounted on foam core and color coded push pins, the production dramaturg outlined the routes between the cities referenced in the text and offered a key with the distances and time of travel. It was also necessary to point out the position of Italian Alps and other geographic obstructions. This concern with passage of time carried over into the first few read-through sessions as the production dramaturg and director went about discerning approximately how many days are covered over the course of the text (ten days) and at what time of day each scene occurs. The time of day question was complicated slightly by the nature of an outdoor performance venue with curtain times of either 7:30 PM or 8:00 PM depending on the day. These two pieces of information impacted not only lighting design choices but also hand prop selection.

The initial sharing of information is usually followed with reading and discussion of the prepared text. During the reading the production dramaturg's most important function is that of active listening for awkward phrases or confusing contextual meanings as well as references that might present difficulties for a particular spectatorship if not clarified by staging.

Img. 4.1 *Taming of the Shrew*. Illinois Shakespeare Festival. Dir.: Catherine Weidner. Photo: R. Lee Kennedy. Petruchio is greeted by Hortensio upon arrival in Padua as Grumio looks on in enjoyment.

Supplementary Remarks from *The Taming of the Shrew*
Illinois Shakespeare Festival
Scott R. Irelan, Production Dramaturg
Catherine Weidner, Director

How fast is your horse?
Walk: Roughly 4 MPH.
Trot: The trot is roughly 9 MPH.
Canter/Lope: (top end) 17 MPH.

City-City	Distance	Walk	Trot	Canter
Padua-Mantua	75 miles	25 hrs	8h15m	4h25m
Padua-Venice	29 miles	7h15m	3hrs	2hrs
Padua-Verona	56 miles	22hrs	6h5m	3h5m
Padua-Pisa	186 miles	47hrs	21hrs	11hrs
Mantua-Verona	28 miles	7hrs	3hrs.	1h55m
Mantua-Pisa	274 miles	43hrs	19hrs	10hrs
Verona-Pisa	190 miles	48hrs	21hrs.	11hrs.

Table Work

Depending on the length of the rehearsal process, a cycle of reading, discussing, and otherwise exploring the text (commonly called table work) may repeat itself multiple times in the first week or two before the actual staging of scenes is initiated by the director. Broadly speaking this is the time when performers spend much of their time dissecting the prepared text for clues to character, story, and motivation. Regardless of whether the show is a classic tragedy by Shakespeare or Kyd or contemporary comedy by Neil Simon or Steve Martin this is the time in a rehearsal process where performers and directors alike expect a production dramaturg to respond quickly, if not instantly, to questions, to offer immediate clarifications, and to suggest possible avenues for exploration within a certain phrase or scene. Given this, table work is both exhilarating and exhausting. The table work portion of rehearsals is so varied and so production-dependent that it is impractical to account for all that will be asked of the production dramaturg. We can, however, offer four guidelines as a basis from which to start this phase, no matter what the venue or the chosen play text:

- Be approachable
- Be concrete, not theoretical or clever;
- Be able to respond in human terms that performers can play in a scene
- Be able to openly admit "I do not know" and try find the answer quickly

While literally sitting around a table is not necessary, what is essential is the ability for performers to come to a fuller understanding of how the words on the page will propel character life on the stage. This means that the production dramaturg must work hard not to be seen as the "text police" but rather as an innovative creative-collaborator who understands the importance of impulse in the rehearsal process.

Advocate for Continuity

Once the tables, literal or metaphoric, have been pushed aside in favor of physical exploration of the text, the production dramaturg usually takes up residence around the director's table somewhere near the assistant director, stage manager or vocal coach. This begins the portion of the process where the production dramaturg will often find the role much quieter, opting for close conversations with the director as opposed to public declarations like those given during the read-through or table work. Often continuity questions are passed to the director (and vice versa) at breaks or through the use of written notes. The urgency of a particular question or note may call for immediate discussion, but it is always wise for the production dramaturg to clarify with the director how best to interject a pressing concern. In most cases, though, there really is no concern or connection that cannot be discussed further at a later point when the performers are on break and out of earshot.

The level to which the production dramaturg is integrated into this physical exploration phase is usually dictated by the artistic director, the company structure, or the director. Nevertheless, there are two "events" in which a production dramaturg should never engage during this period of rehearsals. First, it is not acceptable for the production dramaturg to side-coach performers. Leave that work for the director or any assistants to the director. Second, as discussed earlier, even in many highly collaborative environments it is not necessarily appropriate for the production dramaturg to give notes directly to performers without first passing them by the director. In most cases, we find that it is better to let any and all notes come from the director or an assistant director. What is always suitable, though, is a production dramaturg who is an ardent advocate for continuity. This takes three primary forms:

- For the Production Text: concerned with all elements making sense together
- For the Spectators: concerned with how elements will read to viewers
- For the Performers: concerned with the arc of each character within the given world

Catching directorial inconsistencies or illogical performer choices at this phase of rehearsal often emerges as the primary function of the production dramaturg. These "catches" will save time and stress at a later point in the process, which is why it is so important for the production dramaturg to be present early and often. It is also essential that the production dramaturg remain open to the choices other collaborators are making during the rehearsal process. As many practitioners will attest, conceptual ideas are evolutionary, not set in stone, so what may seem inconsistent to the production dramaturg in early rehearsals might be quite informative as the director works through the whole play. For a production dramaturg who is also functioning as an assistant director, this type of work may carry over into the running of secondary rehearsals.

Runs, Dress-Tech, Preview

As scene-polishing transitions into **run-throughs**, the production dramaturg continues to stand in as an advocate for the three abovementioned areas (production text, spectators and performers). The focus of this advocacy, however, shifts largely to concentrate on the production text and spectatorship. Especially important is a production dramaturg who can use a questioning spirit to clarify the integration and importance of stage fights, hand props, scenery choices, lighting selections, special effects, and sound design. In generating notes, it is a great idea for the production dramaturg to sit in different areas of the theatre space for run-throughs, **dress-technical rehearsals,** and the **preview**. We find it useful, too, to ask the director if there is a specific issue or concern to watch for or listen to during the run. Sometimes the response is as simple as making sure that all of the performers stay spaced on the stage in such a way that much of the house can see and hear them. In other instances, the director might want a production dramaturg to pay attention to how lighting and scenic elements blend together from moment-to-moment to create mood or atmosphere.

The production dramaturg should transcribe rehearsal notes and email them to the director as soon as possible after the run. In the rare case that a production dramaturg and director can meet face-to-face before the next rehearsal, then the email should be supplemented by a hard copy of the notes for the meeting. In our experience it is often better to offer thoughts or concerns in question form rather than declarative statements, because a question to the director about choices invites discussion and collaboration whereas a declarative implicitly sets up an antagonistic face-off. Remember that questions that can be answered with a simple "Yes" or "No" are often unproductive, unless, obviously, an affirmative or a negative response is all the production dramaturg desires to elicit. The curious nature introduced by the production dramaturg within early discussions remains a valuable creative-collaborative tool until opening night. In the following "Complete Works" notes example, the production dramaturg was asked by the director to take notes with the eye (and ear) of an assistant director so simple "Yes" and "No" questions were appropriate. Since many storytelling and continuity issues regarding the NASCAR production conceit had been solved two days before opening night, questions of moment-to-moment execution of the conceit and comic timing were much more important to the director than were notes about character journey or central images of scenes. The provided queries were further teased out in face-to-face conversations with the director prior to the next run.

Excerpted Notes from *The Complete Works of William Shakespeare (abridged)*
Illinois Shakespeare Festival
Scott R. Irelan, Production Dramaturg
Bill Jenkins, Director

<u>Act One</u>

- Can Mark get a house count every night so he can give us that number instead of the generic 400?

- Does Tom mention the NASCAR track they are supposedly at when he first enters from the RV (i.e. Brickyard)?

- Can Tom stay on Mark with the *King John* line delivery?

- Should Tom and Dave get to the "Amen" quicker?

- Does the *Jeopardy* set up of the *Titus Andronicus* "surprise" take too long?

- Why do they have a skull pie in the RV?

- Should Tom search more for the first few lines of the *Othello* bluegrass?

- Did the vocal quality of the comedies section seem weak from where you were?

Planting Seeds of Outreach

When the production dramaturg is able to regularly attend rehearsals and production meetings, it becomes easier for them to begin seeing connections to outreach opportunities that will best serve the live performance event. Whenever possible, questions about lobby display ideas or pre-and-post-show discussions should be taken up with the artistic or managing director during the earliest days of the rehearsal process. Perhaps a conversation about how best to use a website to prepare spectators will transpire. Talks with the director about how the program will be used are also beneficial. Some directors will want to include an introductory note, and others will simply want the character list in a certain order with a short plot synopsis. Whatever the case may be, a production dramaturg can take this information and extend the concern for continuity into often overlooked or underutilized areas, which we address in Chapter Six.

So You Want to be a Production Dramaturg

Because story management is such an amorphous concept that shifts from moment-to-moment, show-to-show, it is important to note that there are probably as many production dramaturgy rehearsal procedures as there are directorial approaches. Indeed, the same director may work radically differently with a production dramaturg depending on the demands of each play text. For example, the director of a university production of *The Taming of the Shrew* wanted the production dramaturg to attend all rehearsals because of the production dramaturg's strong Renaissance theatre background and ability to read Latin. The presence of the production dramaturg was reassuring for the director, who was more accustomed to working on modern political pieces. One year later, the same director invited a different production dramaturg to just a few run-through rehearsals of *Dancing at Lughnasa*, asking them to comment only on the continuity of scenes he had bracketed and highlighted with additional *tableaux* work.

We close Chapter Four, then, with three suggestions that will serve a production dramaturg well in all phases of rehearsals and all levels of involvement:

- Be prepared
- Listen actively, advocate passionately
- Do not take yourself too seriously

The production dramaturg that easily shifts from textual concerns to performance concerns will soon prove a valuable creative-collaborator within the rehearsal process.

An Exercise on Continuity

Practice Checking Consistency

Instructions

1. Choose a classic text that has a filmic version or two, such as *The Tempest*.

2. Read (or re-read) the written text.

3. Watch a recent adaptation. In this case, we prefer *King of California* or Jack Bender's *The Tempest*.

4. While watching, list examples of substitutions.

5. While watching, also consider what sorts of text editing occurred.

   a. Were scenes cut or moved?

   b. What elements of character were emphasized in the film?

   c. Was it set in a particular era?

6. Though filmic versions often bear little resemblance to stage versions of *The Tempest*, the types of details noted during this activity emulate talking about consistencies and inconsistencies noticed when staging a text.

Chapter Glossary

Dress-technical rehearsals: rehearsals in which technical elements such as costumes, lighting and sound are the focus

Formal analysis: a methodology that looks at each constituent part of a play to see how they go together in order to create the play text

Hybrid play: a play text that exhibits structural elements of both Representational Realism and Presentational drama

-ism: a suffix that indicates a theatrical style of production; some examples are Naturalism, Representational Realism, Symbolism, Expressionism, Surrealism, and Absurdism.

Performance text: all elements of a play on stage that can be read by a spectator, much like a text can be read by a reader

Post-modernism: a theatrical style that is marked by its non-linear, collage effect as well as its use of free association and parody

Presentational (non-Illusionistic): both a form and style that is not interested in recreating elements of everyday live but rather in focusing on a theme, idea, or metaphor

Preview: a particular rehearsal wherein select spectators are invited to witness so that the artistic team can get a sense of how the live performance event will be accepted on opening night. When done early enough in the rehearsal process, a preview can offer the chance to adjust portions of the live performance event for clarity and continuity.

Representational Realism (Illusionistic): both a form and style that is interested in recreating elements of everyday life

Run-through: a rehearsal that focuses on running the show (or sequence of scenes) from beginning to end

Chapter Five

The New Play

This chapter suggests ways that a production dramaturg might go about adapting their production dramaturgy skills, gifts and talents when developing newly-written material. Admittedly the role of new play dramaturg is somewhat different both in outlook and approach than that of a production dramaturg for a previously published or produced play, even when carried out by the same individual. We would be remiss to conflate the two. Working on a yet-to-be produced written text with a living playwright presents not only a unique set of challenges but also a matchless sense of achievement when play and playwright are given their due. Appropriately then, we focus this fifth chapter on how the new play dramaturg not only encourages but also facilitates writer-driven continuity.

Finding Works

There are no hard and fast rules about how a new play dramaturg (or the producing organization) goes about making contact with a writer of interest. When working in an academic environment it is often easy to come by a newly-written text because a faculty member (or two) probably specializes in playwriting and has established avenues for not only personal work but also that of their graduate (and perhaps even undergraduate) students to receive public comment. For example, every spring semester at Southern Illinois University Carbondale the Playwright's Workshop produces new student-written plays in its Journeys program. Several of these short plays have gone on to more exposure through the Kennedy Center American College Theatre Festival as well as professional debuts. Colleges and universities with playwriting programs are often affiliated, formally or informally, with professional theatre companies that offer further development opportunities. Within the professional theatre, however, the process is slightly more complex—though there is no dearth of newly-written material from which to choose. Regardless of whether the new play dramaturg is involved in all phases of finding new writers as well as fresh plays, there are two common ways to go about acquiring newly-written texts for production—commissioning and soliciting.

Commissioning and Soliciting

Commissioning a play refers to offering a sum of money in support of a playwright while working on a specific project. Often the broad details of the project are somehow connected to a producing organization's larger artistic vision. In exchange for supporting a writer, the funding theatre frequently asks for the right of first refusal. This means that the producing organization reserves the opportunity to premiere the resulting text created during the period in which the playwright was receiving financial support. Oftentimes, though, the commission never leads to a fully-staged production at the commissioning theatre. If the commissioning theatre passes completely on the new material, then the writer is free to send it out for consideration at other venues.

Soliciting, on the other hand, is a process by which a theatre acquires scripts for consideration without offering a financial incentive, per se. This is often done by placing a call for plays in a trade journal or on a website. In the end, every theatre interested in new works has different policies governing the solicitation process. Similar to commissioning a play, these guiding principles are clearly derived from the producing organization's artistic vision. For example, when soliciting a new musical for the Prince Music Theatre, the dramaturg might call a literary agent to gather some long synopsis material, ten pages of sample dialogue and a demo CD of music for a new piece. At Actors Theatre of Louisville, unproduced full-length plays are accepted primarily from literary agents. However, writers without agents can send a letter of inquiry along with a synopsis and a ten page selection from the script. Similarly, The Citadel Theatre in Edmonton, Alberta predominantly accepts new works directly from playwrights only after an initial letter of inquiry, which must be accompanied by both a writer resume and an indication of whether or not the play has been developed at any other Professional Association of Canadian Theatre venue. No matter what the solicitation process might be at any given venue, decisions by a new play dramaturg (and the producing organization) to proceed with a project or not are frequently based on these types of materials and expectations.

In the long run, most producing organizations use both commissioning and solicitation to find new works, with the literary and dramaturgy personnel playing an integral role in the process.

Evaluating

Assessing scripts, whether commissioned or solicited, is a highly individualized (and admittedly rather subjective) process that is guided not only by the artistic mission of the producing organization but also by the proclivities of the new play dramaturg. In the case of the new musical example above, the next step for the dramaturg would be to listen to the demo to see if it had memorable rhythms and/or lyrics as well as an overarching story that held together. If so, then a call to the writer's agent is in order. We find that when discussing future prospects with an agent, it is helpful to ask a few pointed questions:

- How far along in the creation process are the collaborators?
- Has the material received any sort of comment from public readings?
- Is there a full text available?

And in the case of musicals:

- Is the music arranged/orchestrated already?

Once this process is complete, the dramaturg usually writes a short report on the piece and places it in a literary database. This type of query and filing is helpful when the dramaturg reports back to the producing organization. Knowing how much work is yet to be done on a project directly influences the resources (both time and money) that a producing organization must put behind a project if pursuing it. Given the wide range of material available, the resources needed for each project must be considered separately and dealt with individually. At times this means offering a series of workshops and developmental readings and at others it means staging something right away. Whatever the decision, the new play dramaturg closes this inquiry phase by contacting the writer's agent.

At most theatres dedicated to producing new works, the evaluation of new material follows a much more formal process. For example, at Actors Theatre of Louisville each submission is entered into a main database with writer/agent contact information, cast size and breakdown, a short synopsis and evaluation. There are three full-time staff members in the literary department, as well as two full-time interns and a literary fellow to do this work. The theatre also benefits from having a fleet of former interns who read submissions. In the case of the Humana Festival of New American Plays, readers are looking for material that is newly-written and broadly defined as American. Given this, the literary staff reads roughly 700-900 full-length plays and about 1,500 ten minute plays every year, all of which are reported in the database. All writers or their agents are contacted as well, regardless of outcome. From the pool of submissions, roughly 100 full length plays are discussed further by the artistic staff as serious contenders for the upcoming festival. Once this group of plays is decided upon, the artistic director will listen to pro/con arguments from the literary staff as well as the rest of the artistic staff. There are several points of view, obviously, but in the end, all final decisions on what plays will be included in the festival are made by the artistic director. This process usually leads to the production of six full-length plays, approximately three ten-minute plays and an anthology of short plays commissioned from six or so writers for the apprentice acting company.

The ability to evaluate fresh material is an incredibly important skill for any new play dramaturg to possess. Learning as much about **structure** as well as reading as many plays as possible are fine places to start when developing the "eye" needed to scout new writers and new works. The rest comes with practice. A great way to get practice is to contact professional theatres to see if they have extra plays in their submission pile in need of reading and evaluation. An internship at a **regional theatre** known for producing new work and new writers is also a great way to hone skills as this environment offers personal mentorship.

Establishing Trust

Once a writer's text has been chosen by an organization for either a workshop or production, it is the prime function of the dramaturg working on a new text to establish a safe and trusting atmosphere for the writer. Of course, every playwright and process is different so the new play dramaturg must make sure to clarify what is expected of them by both the playwright and producer(s). A number of playwrights want someone to bounce ideas off of on a daily basis. Others prefer a more hands-off approach. Still others are interested in a little bit of both approaches. In the end, it is the writer's call, so be clear with each other about the creative-collaborative process. The same holds true for the dramaturg's relationship with the director in a new play process. The director must have a relationship with the writer. As such, it is important that the three collaborators talk about hopes, goals and prospects for a workshop or production before getting into the rehearsal room. We recommend drafting a "Letter of Agreement" not unlike what was mentioned earlier if the dramaturg is freelanced into the project. Nonetheless, a dramaturg in either the development process or working on the premiere of new material remains attuned to issues of continuity both in terms of communication and in terms of workshop expectations.

In this setting, the new play dramaturg can create a sense of safety and trust by asking questions rather than posing indictments. Many new play dramaturgs find it useful to read the play through a few times before taking notes and drafting questions. When the dramaturg finally does talk to the playwright, some helpful ways to reflect upon the reading experience include responding to these simple questions:

- What do I like about the play?
- What do I not understand?
- Are there words that I do not know? Why is that?
- Is any character based on a real person? What can I find out about this person?
- Is this story based on real events? What can I find out about these events?
- How does the structure of the play work?

The dramaturg must also take great care to listen to the playwright talk about the new play, rather than vice versa. We turn to "I see" statements as a way to avoid any **prescriptive tendencies**. In the end, it is the new play dramaturg's job to serve the play and the playwright in the best way possible. In light of this, we have found three helpful first questions to ask a playwright:

- Where did you get the inspiration to write this play?
- What would you like to take a deeper look at during the workshop/premiere production?
- What kind of notes would be most helpful for you at this point?

There are certainly more specific questions to ask as the process progresses, but to begin with it is usually best to keep queries simple. We should also note that although a new play dramaturg may think there are "problems" in the play text in need of repair, it is not appropriate to go about telling the writer how to "fix" them. Remember that the playwright always knows the text better than anyone else.

And so...?

An Exercise on Inquiry

This exercise was developed for a dramaturgy seminar session regarding dialogue with a living writer. We use the same techniques and principles when talking to writers in our own new play work.

Instructions

1. Before beginning the exercise it is necessary to either write a two-character piece of about five pages that involves the crumbling of a committed relationship OR seek out a writer to do so.

2. Exchange pieces OR hand out the new material to everyone.

3. Read the text. When done reflect on what was clear and unclear, consider what was enjoyable and not enjoyable and think about how structure does or does not match content.

4. Set up a discussion with the writer, either in a simulated classroom experience or over the phone, in which the new play dramaturg dialogs with the writer. Remember to use "I see" statements as opposed to "You" statements. Consider the list of

questions provided earlier in this chapter.

5. After the conversation, debrief the writer to see what was gained (or lost) from the discussion.

Development

In the early 20th century it was quite common in the US for a new work to be produced "out of town" or as a touring production in preparation for arrival in New York. As the show ran, changes were made. In fact, there are several published accounts describing how book musical writers cut songs, characters and even scenes as the pieces were developed in tryouts. In the last fifty years or so, though, the model for producing new material has changed. Broadway, in particular, is no longer the epicenter of new work that it once was for the likes of Robert Sherwood, Tennessee Williams or even Arthur Miller. Today, some of the best writers have never been produced on Broadway but are considered quite successful by the broader theatre community. So what is being done today to get new material ready for its premiere? Often the material will be given a workshopping opportunity in either a regional theatre or academic environment. In fact, a new piece usually goes through one or more workshops before it gets produced. This said, several plays go through the workshop process without ever seeing a full production.

What is a workshop?

Workshops can take many forms, but the most common approach is to invite a playwright, director, new play dramaturg, group of performers, and a stage manager to meet together at a particular venue to work on a newly-written text. There are workshops that last one day, and others that go on for months. One of the most emulated models in the US is that of the Eugene O'Neill Theatre Center's National Playwrights Conference. Each summer several plays are selected, each is given a few days of rehearsal and then the surrounding community is invited to a **public reading**. Over the course of those few days, performers read through the assigned text several times and ask questions, as do the director and dramaturg; designers are brought in to discuss possibilities for the text if and when it gets a full production, and writers rewrite whatever they see fit. Little about the written text will change over the course of the week, which is, of course, the prerogative of the writer. Regardless of venue, there are three basic workshop tactics commonly used in the US: **first reading**, **cold reading** and **staged reading**. In some instances, a **workshop production** is also part of the development process. Though not necessarily a linear sequence that must be followed, one or more of these developmental strategies is often part of the process of bringing a newly-written text to the stage.

First Reading

This is usually the most informal way of workshopping new material and preparation is often kept at a minimum. In fact, many times scripts are distributed to readers the day of presentation. In an academic setting this might be done in the context of a seminar, with other playwrights reading the material. In the professional world, it may be a group of colleagues sitting in a coffee shop or someone's apartment. Still, in rare cases, either of these venues might offer first readings to the public as a way to preview up-and-coming talent. The aim of this type of workshopping is twofold. First, it allows the playwright to hear how the play sounds. Second, it provides a relatively supportive environment in which to receive feedback.

Cold Reading

In this case, performers with scripts in binders sit at either music stands or at a table and read the play for an invited group of spectators. There is a clear delineation of performer and spectator. The stage directions are read by someone, often a stage manager. Preparation for the cold reading, while more than the informal first reading, is still limited. Even though it varies from venue to venue, the preparation time for a cold reading is usually somewhere around one hour. Though physical movement is not a large part of this session, eye contact between performers is, offering a glimpse at embodied character relationships. The primary purpose of this type of reading is not necessarily to workshop a play but to provide the writer as well as potential producers the opportunity to hear the play read aloud, with the goal of clarifying the overall arc of the plot, understanding character relationships and identifying confusing or irrelevant elements of storytelling that might need to be altered or cut.

Staged Reading

This style of workshop features performers with scripts in hand, the collaborative efforts of a director along with selective set, costume, lighting, and sound elements. Though lines are not necessarily memorized, the staged reading endeavors to emulate a full staging by focusing on dramatic flow and character interactions as much as possible. Rehearsals may last for a few hours or for a week depending on the producing organization. In taking this time, the staged reading also offers the writer ample opportunity to make adjustments to the text right up to the time of the live performance.

Workshop Production

A technique most often used in academic settings, these fully memorized and blocked productions typically have quite a small budget. Set and costumes are normally pulled from stock (if not rehearsal furniture and found clothing) and are adapted to fit the basic given circumstances of the world of the play. Rehearsals can last four to six weeks during which the writer makes adjustments to the text. A post-performance talkback with spectators is frequently included as part of the final process in order to help the writer with revisions.

Final Word on Development

Whether done in a professional or an academic environment, we cannot stress enough that, in all cases, it is up to the playwright to lead the development process. Although there are (rightly) many playwrights' stories about getting stuck in "development hell" or having the script "developed to death", we find that most development experiences are positive for both the play and the playwright. Many texts do end up going through several workshops, so playwrights typically find themselves with several different sets of notes from which to choose revision ideas. The saddest thing for a play is when playwrights lose (or give up) control over their vision by striving to make too many other people happy. A new play dramaturg who has earned the writer's trust can be of great use in avoiding trouble like this by continually checking in with the writer and making sure the writer is always clear about what is wanted from the workshop, while also ensuring that the playwright is empowered to ask for it. The job of a new play dramaturg in this instance, then, is to provide a space where the playwright feels comfortable ignoring notes that are not useful.

Premiere Production

With both lines and blocking memorized, the premiere production provides a writer with the chance to see how the play does "on its feet." Rehearsal can range from a week or two to upwards of six weeks depending on the venue. During this rehearsal time, the writer has multiple opportunities to try out new scenes, characters, dialogue and the like. However, as the performance night approaches the new play dramaturg and director might set a "freeze date" for the writer. Any additions or subtractions after this date are up for negotiation between the writer and the creative team trying to "give life" to the text.

Like other live performance processes, the dramaturg working on new material in performance is part of a team that includes a director, performers, designers, artistic director/producers, stage managers, marketing people and many more. The biggest difference, as mentioned, is that the lead collaborator on the team should be the writer. Given this, the new play dramaturg's primary job remains that of serving both the play and the playwright. If on-staff at the theatre producing the play, then it is part of a dramaturg's job to make sure that everyone, including the stage manager, has the most up-to-date information needed to do their job. Did the playwright cut a character since the last workshop? Then the casting director needs to know. Is there a lot of foul language or a moment of nudity not in a previous draft? Then make sure marketing and group sales are aware. It is also always a good idea to keep the artistic director/producer in the loop on a day-to-day basis.

Before rehearsals, the new play dramaturg should speak with both the writer and the director concerning the goals of this process, how each sees the dramaturg fitting into the process, and how the dramaturg sees the roles they play in the process. With this clarified, the dramaturg needs to go back over the script several times, make a list of questions, and seek out the right moment to ask them before or during table work. With production of a new text comes the added responsibilities of keeping a master script up to date, writing for newsletters and programs from the perspective of someone within the evolutionary process of staging new material, and executing pre-show panels and post-show discussions with spectators and artists about the process. We should note that in our professional work it has been much more common for us to do post-show panels than pre-show discussions. No matter what, before the playwright comes to the theatre to be in residence for rehearsals, it is critical that the new play dramaturg keep the writer aware of what is going at the theatre. This is, obviously, much more important if the writer is not planning to be in residence at all. Whatever the arrangement, it is imperative, especially for a dramaturg who is on staff, to make sure the writer has input, if not approval, of blurbs, articles, lectures, and the like before any of them go public.

When working for a festival of new plays, the skills of any dramaturg are tested. For example, over the course of the recent Humana Festival of New American Plays a single dramaturg worked on three projects simultaneously. In preparing each written text for the rehearsal process, the new play dramaturg collaborated with the writer and marketing department to craft an official blurb as well as an essay for each text to be included in the Humana Festival newsletter. For the first play, both the director and the playwright requested that the dramaturg stay as unfamiliar with the text and the history being depicted onstage as possible so as to offer a "clean impression" of what did and did not make sense while still in rehearsals. The second project was devised by a group of playwrights, none of whom were in residence for rehearsals. The dramaturg communicated mostly by email with them, making fairly specific suggestions for cuts or changes based on what was coming out of rehearsals. On the third piece, the dramaturg was present at an out-of-town workshop several weeks before rehearsals began, and from there through opening, the dramaturg and the director worked closely with the writer to clarify several points in the script. All of the dramaturgs worked closely with both stage management and literary interns to make sure that every change for each of the texts was noted in the master scripts kept in the literary library, which were distributed to designers as needed. In addition to these individualized, writer-centered responsibilities, the dramaturg also attended the weekly meeting with the rest of the artistic staff, where everyone brought each other up-to-date on their rehearsal processes.

Whatever the situation and wherever the venue the new play dramaturg additionally acts as the "eyes and ears" of a producing organization during the production/development process. In this capacity, the dramaturg needs to keep artistic management updated on how the work is going and if there are any ways the organization might be able to help with complications or questions that have arisen. The best producers are typically checking in with all the members of the creative team, not just the dramaturg, in order to ensure a safe and trust-filled environment for the writer.

Public Discussions

Holding a public discussion of new material after a cold reading, staged reading or workshop performance can be an important part of the development process. It is the responsibility of the new play dramaturg to make sure that these discussions are writer-centered opportunities designed to gather useful comments for the revision process. The hope is that, after public comment, the writer will return to the text with the goal of making it stronger, whatever that might mean for them.

Post-Reading Discussions-The "Talkback"

The post-reading discussion, commonly referred to as the "talkback", requires some deliberate preparation so that the dramaturg can not only stay in control of the flow of the conversation but also keep the dialogue on topic and positive for the writer. Before any public reading and subsequent discussion occurs, though, the new play dramaturg must ask the writer what outcome(s) is desired from the process. That is, does the writer actually want critiques and commentary or does the writer simply what to know if the spectators liked the play. If an observation from spectators is the goal, then the dramaturg and writer must work together to create a framework wherein a productive exchange of ideas can occur. If the writer simply wants to know if the spectators liked the play, then the dramaturg should try to convince the writer that a post-show discussion is not needed, because only on rare occasion do all spectators find a new piece fulfilling.

One of the best tasks a new play dramaturg can invite a writer to engage in is the drafting of four or five questions for the session. This writer-generated list often forces writers to reflect upon not only the writing process but also the product in ways that lead to richer revisions after the workshop. It is also wise to let the writer know what type of spectators will be present before drafting questions. If the crowd includes people familiar with talking about new plays in process, then the types of questions are fundamentally different than those asked of persons who rarely see plays, let alone new material. It is also prudent for the dramaturg to ask the writer to think about how the text's strengths and weaknesses might be unpacked in the post-reading time with spectators. This information often aids in transitioning from one series of comments to the next query. As a general rule, we like to have the questions in hand at least twenty-four hours before the reading so that, if need be, we can rephrase questions to allow for focused expressions of ideas. For example, the writer may well ask something like, "Did the ending make sense?" The dramaturg might rephrase that as "What reaction did the ending leave you with exactly?" and "Why do you think that is?" This simple rephrasing allows spectators to more completely own their comments while also allowing the writer to glean viable information for revision. Regardless, writer questions about content are always the best and usually the most helpful after the fact.[1]

It is also important to prepare the spectators for the discussion experience. Before the reading/performance the moderator (often a dramaturg, a literary associate or the artistic director) should state that the material is a work in progress before mentioning a few textual elements to which the writer is interested in hearing responses. Also make it clear that everyone is invited to stay for the post-performance discussion. After the reading/ performance, the new play dramaturg needs to lay down some ground rules. The three we find most helpful are:

- In the interest of not rewriting the play for the writer, respond in "I" statements not "You" statements
- Respond directly to the questions posed by the writer without taking the discussion too far off topic

1   For a more complete discussion consult David Rush, "Talking Back: A Model for Post-performance Discussion of New Plays." *Theatre Topics* 10.1 (2000) 53-63.

- Get to the point sooner rather than later

We often make it clear, too, that the writer will simply take in the comments without defending any writerly choices. However, there are some venues, like Chicago Dramatists Theatre, that encourage writers to engage the questioners. In this case, however, the questioners are usually other writers. Nevertheless, it is vital that the new play dramaturg clarify with the writer whether there will or will not be any direct dialogue with respondents. Regardless of venue, the response sessions we have guided often follow a basic format once the ground rules are set:

- Open with an icebreaker question like: "Who wants to tell us, in one word/sentence, what the play was about for them?"
- Transition into and follow the writer's questions
- Redirect any abusive or off-topic comments
- Ask what patterns spectators heard or noticed
- Close with a thank you and invitation back

We generally try to keep the talkback at somewhere around fifteen to twenty-five minutes. The final step in the process for a new play dramaturg is to debrief the writer at a later date, focusing on what was learned about the material not only from the workshop experience but also from the public comments.

Post-Production Discussion

By the time new material finds its way into production, the ground rules for a post-show discussion change slightly. Often these discussions are less about the writer seeking comments regarding plot, character, language or spectacle and more about presenting a panel of creative-collaborators talking about their work on the premiere of a show. In these cases, the new play dramaturg still consults with the writer beforehand concerning a format for the talkback, but the flow is usually much less formal than that of developmental discussions. For example, when working on a new play at the Boston Playwrights' Theatre, the dramaturg and writer agreed that the session should be more about spectators asking questions of the creative-collaborative team. This was decided largely because the text had been already through two rather rigorous academic workshop processes at both Southern Illinois

University Carbondale and Boston University. In addition, it had garnered multiple recognitions within the Kennedy Center American
College Theatre Festival, and now a professional debut. Given this, the
twenty minute interchange followed a rather rudimentary format:

- Basic ground rules (i.e. allotted time, question types, etcetera)
- Introduce the panelists. Do not wait for performers
- Begin the discussion with the director and other panelists while
  awaiting the arrival of performers
- Introduce the performers as they arrive
- Facilitate dialogue, rephrasing any spectator questions or col-
  laborator responses that sound convoluted, confusing or con-
  founding
- Close with a thank you to spectators and artists alike
- Start the applause

It is also a good idea to "hang around" after the session not only to
continue interacting with spectators who still have questions but also
to act as a gatekeeper to those spectators who might be monopolizing
an artist's time or hounding them for an autograph.

So You Want to be a New Play Dramaturg

New material and productions of new material are prepared in so
many different ways that this chapter is only the start of a much longer
learning process. Ultimately, a practiced new play dramaturg becomes
known for the skill to collaborate differently and appropriately on every project that comes along. Our work as new play dramaturgs mirrors
many of the processes and skills mentioned in previous chapters.

Two of the most significant attributes of a dramaturg working on
new material in development and production are those of flexibility
and openness. Serving the play and playwright should not be a passive
job. Be aware that a good chunk of the process involves both diplomacy
and patience. In addition, always remember that just because a new
play dramaturg does not understand something the director is doing or
agree with an angle that a playwright is working on does not mean that
anyone is wrong. Ask questions, have an opinion, be supportive and
find a way into the exciting process of collaborating on new material.

Chapter Glossary

Cold reading: this type of development process features performers with scripts in binders sitting at either music stands or at a table while they read for an invited group of spectators

Commissioning: when a producing organization offers a playwright a sum of money to sustain work on a specific project, usually tied to some sort of overarching theme or artistic vision

First reading: This is the least formal type of development process and features a group of colleagues and/or friends meeting in an informal setting such as a coffee house to read the new material for the writer.

Prescriptive tendencies: predispositions that a creative-collaborator might hold in regards to telling a writer how to "fix" or "better write" play material

Public reading: a general notion that refers to the process of speaking new material in a freely available area, whether someone's apartment or an actual theatre space, so that a writer can hear the new text interpreted by others

Regional theatre: a not-for-profit professional theatre that produces a season of plays fit for the region it serves (i.e. The Guthrie in Minneapolis)

Soliciting: a process by which a theatre acquires scripts for consideration by placing a call in a trade publication or online

Staged reading: This type of developmental process features performers with scripts in hand that have been aided by the collaborative efforts of a director, which may also include selective set, costume, lighting, and sound elements.

Structure: referencing elements of a text that indicate whether or not it is climactic or episodic in plot as well as considering what the point of attack, crisis moment and resolution of the text might be as written

Workshop production: This type of developmental process features the memorization of lines and blocking as well as budget-restricted costume, set, sound and light design.

PART THREE
In Production

This third section of *The Process of Dramaturgy* points to ways in which the information gathered in Section One and the tasks outlined in Section Two converge as a production makes its way towards its opening night and scheduled run. Most often this coming together is in the form of outreach and education endeavors (broadly defined). Though a majority of professional theatre companies are equipped with education departments in charge of outreach activities, these departments are often not as familiar with the director's vision for the live performance event as is the production dramaturg. In this case the production dramaturg serves as liaison between the education department and the production. In academic theatre settings, outreach functions often fall by the wayside or are taken on by a faculty member or student only indirectly attached to the live performance event. The production dramaturg is often the only connection to continuity in these situations. Ideally marketing and public relations efforts will be tied into the overall storytelling that will appear on stage. Whether in professional or academic theatre this proves to be a challenge—a challenge, however, that a production dramaturg can aid in meeting if given the opportunity to do so.

Chapter Six reviews ways in which the cumulative work of the production dramaturg might convey itself in the program, express themes and ideas through community dialogue, and engage spectators via interactive lobby displays. Chapter Seven is a case study narrative that offers an example of how all the factors mentioned within this book might ideally come together over the course of pre-production, rehearsals, and in production. We close *The Process of Dramaturgy* with some thoughts for instructors and student dramaturgs.

Chapter Six

Outreach and Education

This chapter emphasizes how the work of a production dramaturg both in preparation and in rehearsal can express itself through a variety of activities and publications that extend notions of continuity to engage spectators before they arrive at the live performance event and often after the event itself. This succinct look at possible avenues for outreach and education is meant to encourage conversations between the production dramaturg and the producing organization on ways in which both might better serve the spectatorship. As we have emphasized throughout our discussions, every production has its idiosyncrasies. There are, though, general practices that can assist in establishing and maintaining strong community relations. In a professional venue where there is a marketing department, outreach concerns often fall under the purview of marketing or group sales, but in an educational setting the production dramaturg may be called upon to work to this end with the box office and marketing. Based on not only the best practices of our own work but also that of other LMDA practitioners, we hope that the ideas presented here will be duplicated, tested and enhanced.

Resource Packet and Study Guides

Providing learners at all levels with access to live performance has great value and can go a long way to fostering inquiry, especially when there is solid preparation offered in some sort of learning environment. In larger professional venues, with entire departments devoted to educational outreach, the production dramaturg will have only an indirect (if any) involvement in the compilation of resource materials for teachers, students or other spectator groups. In either academic theatre or smaller professional companies, however, the production dramaturg will undoubtedly be engaged in the preparation of materials for special matinees or events surrounding the live performance.

Happily, the tasks involved in generating resource packs and study guides often overlap with the production dramaturg's pre-production research and assembly of materials for the artistic team. Accordingly, crafting outreach publications need not be inordinately time-consuming. In fact, both the dramaturg's production book and production resource pack contain a great deal of material appropriate for teachers and students preparing to attend a given live performance. Thus, much of the information-gathering involved in creating educational resource packs or study guides is completed as part of other production dramaturgy preparations. The production dramaturg can cull from this existing material, with an eye toward age-appropriateness and writing style, a rather extensive outreach publication. For example, information on past productions or recommendations of film versions of the play text that are not necessarily suitable to share with performers are often helpful for teachers in preparing lesson plans or community groups bringing a busload of patrons. In essence, then, the production dramaturg finds ways to utilize some "outtakes" from earlier research endeavors in the outreach process.

When working with K-12 institutions it is important that a production dramaturg remember that many schools do not include drama as a regular part of their curriculum. Given this, the production dramaturg ought to incorporate information, discussion questions, and activities that appeal to teachers of History, English, Science, and other disciplines relevant to the production at hand. In short, give teachers as many ideas as possible without overwhelming them. In our experience, teachers welcome this type of supplementary material. Moreover, busy teachers appreciate specific lesson plans. Of course, tone is important, and the material must be presented in a professional and collegial manner. The lesson plan should encourage teachers to connect the production with an existing learning environment as well as excite student learning about theatre and live performance. The plans should not alienate anyone with a condescending style. Most importantly, include material that is pertinent to the production they will see. For example, the Study Guide for *Our Town* included an activity that used miming the use of everyday objects as well as images that appeared in the production as a way to prepare young spectators for their experience. Other best practices when assembling teacher resource pack include:

- Realizing schools have varying resources, so quote (with appropriate citations) from important sources and point teachers toward DVDs they might rent at a low cost
- Pointing teachers toward reputable web sites like the Library of Congress, Folger Library, etc., that offer archives of still and moving images
- Creating a combination of literature or writing-based discussion questions and hands-on activities
- Including visuals that directly influenced production design choices as well as final versions of designer material. This is best done as a CD-Rom or DVD. In professional environments both unionized designers and performers must agree to all such representation and presentation of their work.

Whether meant for an educational institution or community group, outreach and educational resources should include discussion topics for both pre- and post-production. For example, a post-show prompt for *My Fair Lady* at Actors Theatre of Louisville asked spectators to reflect on which women in the musical were portrayed as "weak" and which as "strong", before leading into a discussion of Eliza's transformation as it related to the live performance. Ideas generated during this dialogue easily transition into a consideration of Shaw's *Pygmalion* and its possible Feminist undertones.

Typically, those attending special performances appreciate receiving material well in advance. An early mailing announcing the dates of special performances designed for students or community groups should include information concerning resource materials that will be made available. Additionally, if the producing organization maintains a web site, then all outreach and education materials should be posted for potential spectator groups to utilize.

Study Guide Table of Contents for *Our Town*
Southern Illinois University Carbondale
Maureen Conway, Production Dramaturg
Lori Merrill-Fink, Director

Our Town
Study Guide
Table of Contents

Program Material

Once spectators have arrived at the theatre, one of the most valuable outreach resources available to the production dramaturg is the program. Though production dramaturgs have little input into the design, layout, or overall content of the program, they can reinforce issues of continuity in the way that they utilize their allotted space within the publication. The most common ways we go about this include the program note, the interview, the synopsis, and the cast of characters listing.

Program Note

Perhaps one of the more recognizable dramaturgical contributions to a live performance event, the program note is probably the most important outreach element available to the production dramaturg. As a rule of thumb, the program note contains information directly related to the production and is presented in a form that can be digested in five minutes, which is the average time a spectator has between their arrival and the start of the performance. It may also be useful to think of it as information patrons will enjoy after the show, when they have time to read the program. A production dramaturg should never count on patrons reading the note prior to a live performance in order to gain a better understanding of the play. For our purposes here, we identify four loosely-defined categories: *Antagonistic, Historical, Textual,* and *Production.*

The antagonistic note works in concert with the director's note to create a dialogue about issues of concept or agenda. The advantage of this style of note is that whether it is read before or after seeing the production, it has the potential to open a variety of pathways to understanding. The obvious disadvantage is that if not clearly contextualized, the antagonistic note may not always foster further discussion of what appears on stage. In contrast, the historical note brings to the fore moments in a particular historical narrative that are relevant to the era in which the play was written as well as the period in which the production is set. The advantage here lies in the ability of the production dramaturg to share interesting pieces of information from the "hunting and gathering" phase. The dangerous disadvantage with this note is an (often unintended) anachronistic or myopic perception of the use of history within the production. Similar in tendency but concentrating on the play-as-literature, is the textual note. The advantage to this form of program note is that it embraces the literary qualities of a given script, often highlighting important themes or metaphors. The disadvantage is that it only perfunctorily addresses production elements, frequently coming off as distant in tone and excessively literary. Then again, the pragmatics of creating a program for an entire season necessitates the use of a textual note more often than not because the program's publication deadline is usually long before each production begins rehearsals. By and large, the production note talks about issues in the context of the play onstage. At its best, the production note calls attention to particular elements to watch or listen for during the live performance. At its worst, the production note reads as a lengthy end-note, spelling out choices and how a spectator should interpret them. Given all this, some of the best program notes are those that blend aspects of all four types.

As a production dramaturg considers the form and content of the note, it is also important to keep in mind issues of style. Obviously the subject matter of the dramaturgical note, regardless of whether it is 250 words or 2,050 words in length, should illuminate the live performance in some way. At the same time the production dramaturg must be conscious that the contents of the piece can confuse the logic of a live performance if it is too cerebral, disjointed, or otherwise jammed with jargon. There are a few "tricks" we find helpful in avoiding these pitfalls. First, think of the program note as a pressing journalism story that must be told. Second, take a conversational tone and tenor comparable to that which is found in *USA Today*, the *Chicago Tribune*, or the like. Third, try to point to production-relevant issues, whatever those may be, without giving away too much. With this in mind, we loosely structure the piece as follows:

- With implied "I see" statements, write a **soft lead** rather than a **hard lead** (see Chapter Glossary)
- Follow up with a transition that establishes tone (see abovementioned)
- Turn to a narrative that tells the story using chosen tone and tack
- Close with summation and tie back to soft lead

The program note that must encompass an entire season of plays follows much the same format. Obviously, the challenge for any production dramaturg in this instance is to provide a balanced view of each chosen play while also thematically linking them and reinforcing season unity. In the subsequent newsletter article excerpt, notice how the comedic tone of the soft lead and transition paragraph matches the comedic tone of the play text and its subsequent performance. All of these considerations also come into play when the production dramaturg drafts a newsletter essay, which is usually sent out well in advance of the live performance event.

When feasible, the production dramaturg needs to have access to the director's note prior to writing the dramaturgical note. This is important for two reasons. First, it allows the production dramaturg to better choose what type of note to compose. Second, much like other journalistic endeavors, it provides an opportunity to edit the tone and tenor of both publications in a way that best serves the publisher, in this case the producing organization. We should note that there are occasions when the production dramaturg may even be asked to "ghost write" a note for the director.

Newsletter Articles

Though related to the program note in content, the newsletter article can and should be more expansive and philosophical because it is introducing the style of the play to subscribers. Since patrons already have tickets, a production dramaturg need not necessarily "sell it" to them. As such, the production dramaturg need only to share excitement about the upcoming live performance event. In the example below, note how the production dramaturg fits the tone of the article to the tone of the play text while still relaying vital information.

Newsletter Article Excerpt from *The Underpants* (adapted from *Die Hose*)
Actors Theatre of Louisville
Julie Felise Dubiner, Production Dramaturg
BJ Jones, Director

> *I just flew in from Munich, and boy! Are my arms tired!*

> *Did you hear the one about the Hamburger and the Frankfurter?*

"Funny" is not so much the word that springs to mind when one thinks "German", but there is such a thing as German Comedy and Carl Sternheim was a master of it. Born in 1878 to an assimilated Jewish father and an equally non-religious

Lutheran mother (setting him up for a lifetime of religious confusion), Sternheim studied law and philosophy, served in the cavalry, and wanted to be a writer. Luckily his second wife was a well-read heiress who recommended he look at the French Neo-classic writer, Molière, who proved to be a great inspiration (despite being badly translated).

Sternheim's plays were first produced in the years leading up to World War I, and were considered both tremendously scandalous and totally hilarious. *Die Hose*, from which Steve Martin radically adapted *The Underpants*, was the first part of a tetralogy of plays about the Maske family. It was banned by the censors for its salacious title and content, but was allowed to go on in 1911 after the title (but not the content) was changed to *Der Reise* (*The Giant*). Sternheim took a hard look at the ridiculousness of the increasingly powerful middle class, of which he was guilty of being a member. He titled the published collection of his plays *Aus dem bürgerlichen Heldenleben*, which translates as *From the Lives of Bourgeois Heroes* (you may insert your own joke here)....

Through the 19th and 20th centuries, comedy inched its way back into German culture, most often tucked into political satire. The Expressionist movement is not usually referred to as a laugh riot, but it was at its height when Carl Sternheim was writing. Although he considered his risqué satires realistic, his plays and novels often are categorized as Expressionistic due to their spare language and skewed and skewering critique of contemporary Germany. Some Theatregelehrte consider his style a bridge between the abject Sexualität and Gewalttätigkeit in the Vorexpressionistischen Werke of Frank Wedekind (whose daughter was his third wife) and the Nachexpressionistischen combination of Musikhalle and moralism of Bertolt Brecht and the wild und verrückt concept of Verfremdungseffekt. Sorry, that got a little serious (although, as you can see, when not tied down by grammar rules, it is a pretty funny language)...

Now, have you heard the one about the civil servant's wife whose underwear falls down during a parade?

— Julie Felise Dubiner

The Interview

Though style, form, and function vary drastically, the interview is a valuable way to reinforce aspects of continuity as well. In our experience, there seem to be four over-arching categories of interviews: *Artist, Behind the Scenes, Genre-Specific*, and *Hard News*. The artist interview is almost certainly the most familiar to theatre patrons. These interviews normally highlight the work of a director, fight master, performer, writer, or designer. The questions posed are intended to be a fast, easy way for artists to reveal their perspective, work habits, quirks, and the like. This can also be the place where the artist in question may well promote a particular cause or mention previous and future work at a particular venue. It is the responsibility of the production dramaturg, though, to make sure that all published questions and responses, to some extent, concern the play-in-performance.

Somewhat related but broader in scope is the Behind the Scenes interview. These commonly turn to members of the technical staff (props, scenery, lighting, costumes, special effects, stage manager) as a person of interest. What makes this type of interview enjoyable for a production dramaturg is the way that the responses put forward can lead to a fascinating discussion of "theatrical magic" that few spectators even think about when watching a live performance. The genre-specific interview is just that. Used most effectively with comedy, especially farce, the production dramaturg typically works closely with the director to produce an interview, hypothetical or actual, that captures the spirit of the live performance. Hard News interviews frequently engage members of the artistic administration in a discussion about the producing organization. These interviews are rarely the purview of the production dramaturg. However, in smaller companies or in educational settings the production dramaturg may be the best prepared and most aware individual available for the task.

While the processes of preparing, conducting and transcribing interviews are beyond the scope of this book, we do offer some guidelines to consider:

- Questions should be short, simple and specific to the production
- Avoid posing "closed" questions that can be answered "yes" or "no"

Genre-Specific Interview from *Complete Works of William Shakespeare (abridged)*
Illinois Shakespeare Festival
Scott R. Irelan, Production Dramaturg
Bill Jenkins, Director

I caught up with "Complete Works" Director Bill Jenkins at a rehearsal shortly after Memorial Day. He was still recovering from a bout with rubbery cheese curds (are there any other kind), but he was kind enough to offer these reflections on the play, his directing, and the metaphysics of comedy.

What is your favorite word in "Complete Works"?
Hmmmm.....I would have to say my favorite lines would be "We don't have to do it justice. We just have to do it!"

What is your least favorite line or word in "Complete Works"?
Coriolanus. I find it offensive.

Really? What about that is offensive to you?
[Censored] … THAT's what I find offensive about it.

Holy cow! Well...moving right along then, what about this play gets you going creatively, spiritually or emotionally?
I like to laugh...and I like to see other people laugh. I think, probably more than anything, seeing people release the pressures of their life and just laugh for two hours is the greatest joy I can imagine as a director....unless they are laughing during a production of *Hamlet* or *Death of A Salesman* that I might direct....that would be a bad thing.

I often find that Shakespeare's comedies are not half as funny as his tragedies.
COME ON! You took that line straight from the show.

Sorry bro. I couldn't help myself. It makes so much sense that I just had to repeat it. So, what about this play makes you shut down creatively, spiritually or emotionally?

The actors.....they are very limited and not funny at all. It is a big problem. Hopefully, the play can be salvaged through funny props and costumes. PROPS! PROPS! PROPS! (This, by the way, is sarcasm).

Since you mentioned funny, what piece of staging makes you laugh so hard you cry?

Any fight sequence choreographed by DC Wright.

Nice. What piece of staging makes you cry so hard you have to laugh?

Anything that I have blocked...how in the heck did I get a degree in this?

What is your favorite swear word to motivate the performers?

I don't swear...I am an Irish Catholic.

No wonder you need to laugh. Let's see...What profession besides directing would you be willing to attempt?

Television commentator for the Chicago Cubs. Go Cubbies!

Now that you mention it, that does sound like fun. Okay then, what profession besides directing would you totally refuse to think of trying?

Swimsuit Model (this is a major blow to many, I know)

Last but certainly not least, rarely read and little studied Roman ethnomusicologist Nocens Aduro Maximus comments in his "Sanus Incuratus Graecorum" (Tone Deaf Greeks) that the sounds of a play—jejune or otherwise—are much more important than the spoken words. Is this true of your approach to "Complete Works" or do you find your work to be a little more nuanced than what Nocens Aduro Maximus suggests?

Due to my education, I do not understand anything you have just asked.

Fair enough.

— Scott R. Irelan

- Try using prompts like "explain", "describe", "why", or "how"
- Chat with the interviewee before getting to your questions to set an appropriate tone for the task at hand
- Consider emailing general topics of interest beforehand so the interviewee has a chance to "prepare"
- When editing for space, ask what the spectators would most want to know, and include that regardless of personal preference.

In the end the most important element of an interview for the program is relevance to continuity.

Synopsis and Cast of Characters Listing

Not often considered an essential print component of production dramaturgy, both the synopsis and cast of characters listing provide the production dramaturg another opportunity to reinforce unity. We should note that when working with Equity performers, there are points of interest regarding the cast of characters listing that may need to be contractually negotiated. Although those negotiations are the responsibility of the managing director or general manager and not the production dramaturg, it is wise to check on specifics before beginning the writing process. Character listings also may be dictated by prior agreement (i.e. for musicals, "chorus" roles and "principal" roles are important distinctions; and some performers may have in their contracts with the producing organization how and where they must be listed).There are a variety of perspectives on the use and function of the **program synopsis**. Several practitioners find them to be tedious exercises that remove all sense of mystery from the play-in-production. Some find them to be, in general, a cause of confusion rather than an aid to clarity. Still others believe that a lengthy program synopsis is a crutch for those with a short attention span. We find, however, that a well-crafted and concise program synopsis is useful. To create one, we carefully consider the following fundamental questions:

- What is the story of the play? Not plot point by plot point but in terms of mood, relationships and conflict.
- What is production-specific to the story of the play?
- What does a spectator absolutely need in order to make sense of

the world of the play-in-production? In other words, what can be left out while still offering clarification?

• How can I do this in 150-300 words?

It is always a good idea to engage the director in a discussion regarding the synopsis. In most instances an editorial eye and sense of the overall story of the play will strengthen the piece.

The cast of characters listing is a great way to compliment the synopsis because it offers a place not only to provide descriptors of each character but also to highlight relationships. Some considerations include:

• What order do the characters arrive on stage; or which character pair is the story about exactly?

• How are the characters related to one another, if at all?

• Where do the characters come from when first we meet them?

This too should be addressed with the director to ensure that the format best suits the production vision. Admittedly, some directors will not care. It has been our experience, though, that if given the chance the director enjoys extending an artistic expertise to these types of endeavors.

Ultimately, both the program and newsletter material are vital communicative tools that ought to enhance and enliven a spectator's experience as opposed to dictating or determining it for them.

Pre-Show Programming and Post-Show Discussions

Most of what the production dramaturg generates for the above-mentioned undertakings is quite useful when interacting directly with spectators either before or after a live performance. Sometimes these interactions are in-school visits or community engagements at a luncheon given in preparation for a group excursion. For the most part, however, preshow and post-show activities are conducted just ahead of or immediately after the live performance at the theatre proper. In general the preshow lecture should concern itself with issues of the play-as-literature, only slightly pointing to production elements (if at all) while the post-show discussion ought to be about issues that arise within the live performance of the play text. However, if there is only to be one oral presentation of ideas—and often that is a pre-show lecture—it might be wise to find a way to discuss literary aspects of the script while also pointing to how they specifically manifest themselves in the live performance.

Pre-show programming—whether a lecture or panel of experts—is an intriguing challenge for a production dramaturg because of the vast range of experiences and theatrical knowledge of those in attendance. Given this, it is helpful to choose one main avenue of inquiry and explore that as fully as possible. Whatever this may be, much of the time should be spent focusing on this chosen area of interest. We like to limit our time to twenty or thirty minutes, with about five minutes or so for questions. We have found that patrons tend to prefer arriving closer to curtain time, so the pre-show programming can lead them right to their seats ready to focus on the performance event at hand. The use of notes is absolutely appropriate and a great way to stay within an allotted time frame. The talk should be full of striking and complex ideas that are presented in everyday vernacular, a tone not unlike that of the evening news or daily newspaper. The use of moving images, still photos or even pieces of music are a great way to get the patrons interested in the subject matter at hand. Whatever the production dramaturg chooses to share with patrons, it is never a good idea to synopsize the play or directly address production choices. For example, a discussion before *Our Town* might address how the play has been marginalized or "de-anthologized" over time and why that is. For *My Fair Lady*, perhaps the preshow time is spent outlining the evolution of musical theatre in the US from its European roots to late-20th century innovations, playing some music or showing clips from film versions of musicals. The possibilities are often endless, constrained largely by time and resources.

The post-show discussion is customarily the place where production-specific topics are investigated. At times, this might be the venue where artists (director, performers, designers, or even the writer) discuss "heavy" issues brought out by the production. More times than not, though, this is a light-hearted conversation between spectators and artists, to which the production dramaturg often plays onlooker. If the production dramaturg has the chance to insert personal thoughts, then a spectator has probably posed a question that no one wants to respond to or has no idea how to field. Two of the more common questions seem to be "How do you memorize all those lines?" and "I watched the movie before coming and was wondering what influence it had on this production?" While it is wholly appropriate to answer with something like "With practice" and "Not at all", the production dramaturg should seize the moment as one of education. Since the point of having these types of discussions is to cultivate and sustain spectators, it is better to redirect these types of surface inquiries to those much more related to theatrical meaning-making in production than to dismiss them out of hand. The post-show discussion also provides a production dramaturg with the unique chance to listen to what patrons found confusing and what they found clear. This feedback, though production-specific, can go a long way toward the planning of future outreach events.

Lobby Display

The spectatorial experience begins as soon as individuals enter the theatre facility, and, as such, they should be actively engaged as soon as possible. This early involvement must extend the world of the live performance beyond the theatre space and draw spectators into the production at hand. Given this aim, there are basically three types lobby display designs: *Interactive, Experiential* and *Educational*. Time and again in our professional work, lobby display designs are partially dictated by both the public relations and front of house departments, which usually require material fit a standard size, format and place-ment. These requirements have repeatedly been much more relaxed in our academic work. Often with standardization comes not only less person-hours invested in mounting the lobby display but also more of a budget for materials. Though we isolate the design types here as a point of discussion, more often than not, each type is used in combination to create a relevant experience for spectators. In general, all lobby designs offer production-oriented information that best captures the spirit of the live performance in addition to ideas and themes inherent to the play text. The trick, as it were, is selecting and the creating a balance of written text, image(s) and aural material that not only draws spectators into the venue but also keeps them engaged with the production itself. As in the design of museum exhibitions, any placard text should be in a large, easily readable font. Since most spectators will be drawn in by images, the amount of text to read should be limited.

The **interactive lobby display** is one that invites participants to engage materials at their own leisure, often offering them the opportunity to conduct a self-guided tour with a headset, play a short DVD or CD, listen to music from the production, or perhaps even write or draw a response to subject matter linking the lobby material to the play text, everyday life and the live performance. The **experiential lobby display** is much the same. The difference, though, lies in the extent to which live bodies other than those of spectators are employed to engender a visceral response to the world of the production. For *Death and the King's Horseman*, for example, a stationary Yoruba market place composed of booths with Nigerian baskets, onions, gourds, cowry beads, etcetera was created and a display of authentic headdresses and other artifacts was added. Volunteers in traditional Nigerian garb wandered the lobby. This naturally blended with the opening moments of the production and blurred normalized boundaries between spectators and performers, lived reality and the world of the play. Frequently with the experiential lobby design, the preshow music is piped into the entrance space (along with, in rare instances, the smells of the world of the production) so that there is an even clearer link between the live performance and spectator experiences. The simplest of the three designs, the **educational lobby display** is just that, educational. In this case much of the materials exhibited offer a broad view of the processes inherent to staging the live performance. For example, the light plot with accompanying color filters and patterns, the scenic designer's ground plan and model, and the costume renderings are exhibited. Each of these is accompanied with a brief artistic statement and set of inspirational images. Showing these also allows production dramaturgs to display their work in the form of books, images and brief statements of information drawn from the production resource pack. No matter what design style is ultimately used, the challenge always lies in selecting the appropriate lobby display for the production at hand, budgetary constraints aside. We should note,

Img. 6.1 *The Crucible*-A Guard searching bags as part of the experiential lobby experience. McLeod Theatre. Dir.: OleSegun Ojewuyi. Lobby design conceived by set designer Brad Carlsen and A.D. Jenny Holcombe. Photo: Robert Holcombe.

too, that the time invested in mounting a lobby display is directly related to the type chosen. An educational display, for example, may take two to four hours to complete whereas an interactive-experiential display may take a minimum of six hours to finish. In one instance, a student production dramaturg elected to emphasize Thornton Wilder's contrast in *Our Town* between the smallest details of daily life (micro) and the vastness of the universe (macro). The proposed lobby display included images of the galaxies and historical quotations that referenced humankind's place in the cosmos. When working on *A Raisin in the Sun*, a student production dramaturg decided to focus on how the play still resonates for residents of South Chicago and utilized recently published newspaper articles about housing in the area to generate an educational/interactive lobby design.

An Exercise on Outreach and Education

Devising a Lobby Display Ground Plan

Instructions

1. Select one of the plays mentioned thus far.

2. Read the play with an eye toward developing a lobby design. Presume your target spectators are coming from a college/university community.

3. Starting with the educational lobby design, develop a ground plan for the layout as well as sample materials.

4. Make adjustments to your initial ideas and create an educational lobby display, and then devise an interactive lobby design. Consider how this changes your ground plan.

5. Make adjustments to these ideas to make the lobby design experiential. Consider how this changes your ground plan.

6. Placing the ground plans and materials next to each another, compare the positives and negatives of each lobby design.

A Larger Dialogue

Developing a symposium is a great way to expand the dialogue about themes and issues related to a given play text. The following is a series of suggestions that have worked best for us regardless of the venue:

- Connect the symposium to a relatively familiar play text or period of history dealt with in the season of plays.
- Formulate a guiding question or theme.
- Assess availability of resources both financial and human.
- Inform as many colleagues as possible and invite them to participate.
- Invite outside practitioners and scholars with expertise in something related to the guiding question or theme.
- Devise ways to involve the broader community and develop education materials accordingly.

- Revise curricular preparations as the event grows nearer so that a larger population from the community will feel prepared and welcomed.

- Generate ways for interested patrons to interact with invited guests and symposium presenters so as to foster an inviting learning environment.

- Invite the symposium guests to attend the live performance event together, perhaps engaging in a pre-show talk or post-show discussion.

- Debrief to experience to see what can be done better the next time.

- Publish and present the preparation and outcomes of the event.

Whether a production dramaturg is working within a regional theatre, small not-for-profit house, or academic theatre setting, these steps can be amended or expanded as needed. For example, an academic theatre production of *Our Town* became the genesis for a larger discussion about marginalized voices of 1920s and 1930s US theatre and live performance.

Given the somewhat checquered history of *Our Town* both as a text and in performance, organizing a symposium around the idea of "giving voice" to marginalized voices seemed appropriate. Taking place over three days, the event included six panel presentations, two one-person performances, a keynote address, an all-symposium dinner, and attendance at the live performance event. In addition, course syllabi for Theatre History, Theatre Insights (an introductory level class) and Play Analysis were adapted to fit the symposium theme. A US Drama Special Topics class was developed as well. Part of the lobby display for this production included samples of in-class exercises from the introductory level class. Both of the exercises below were developed to personalize the play for students who often have had little to no exposure to dramatic literature or live theatrical performance. They have since been shared with participants at the First International Thornton Wilder Conference, where they appeared in a packet distributed to educators. These written exercises worked well in conjunction with a guided imagery exercise in which individuals close their eyes and [re]imagine their favorite place in great detail. Then they imagine leaving it. Utilizing Uta Hagen-like sense memory exercises that engage all five senses, individuals improvised a "Goodbye" monologue inserting their own list of items to which they would bid farewell. Next, they performed Emily's final monologue from the final act of the play and discussed the similarities and differences.

"My Town"

Instructions

Through the use of personal narrative, write a one-page description, in monologue form, of your hometown as if you were the Stage Manager describing the layout. For those who have grown up in a large urban center like Chicago, this activity is asking for description of immediate neighborhood surroundings.

> Example: "My town is a rough place to live. There are dangerous people just walking the streets. The corner is in the middle of the block. It has a big red door that you come in and out of. My house is on the edge of the block. We have an American flag hanging outside the house. The building was painted brown a few years ago. The street is big and wide. I see many people outside doing negative things on the streets. I'm glad I moved away from my town."

"My Goodbye"

Instructions

Through the use of personal narrative, write a one- page description, in monologue form, of things and people in your life to which you would bid adieu if you were in the same position as Emily Webb in Act Three. This exercise asks you to pay particular attention to descriptive language that uses all five senses.

> Example: "…Smell of my daughter's lotion after her bath, the nights my husband and I talk about nothing and our talks about everything, dinners in, dinners out, relaxing vacations."

Public Relations and Marketing Materials

Another area in which a dramaturg can make a wonderful contribution is in public relations and marketing materials. Much of what the production dramaturg generates for other facets of the production process might be well-suited for these varied outreach materials. In our experience it is worth the effort for a production dramaturg to develop a non-adversarial relationship with both the public relations and marketing departments. We have found a great way to do this is by offering to write blurbs for the season shows, articles for newsletters and program material. We have also helped write press releases, edited written materials for brochures as well as newsletter articles/program notes we have not written. In some instances, we have even been on standby to answer questions as marketing plans are developed. This said, it is important not to infringe on their expertise, providing services only when requested.

One of the most useful channels of communication is a website, the use of which is nearly limitless. Though web design is outside the realm of this book, we do recommend that even the most basic production dramaturgy segments of a website include a synopsis of the play that focuses on information not included in the program, an author biography with life-elements that directly relate to the play, and some sort of historical context document. When given more room, other materials might include:

- Artist blog about the process
- Uploaded short interviews with artistic staff
- Questions to think about before and after the live performance event
- Classroom learning resources
- Crossword, word search, or other gaming opportunities tied to text.

It goes without saying that regardless of what finally appears on the production dramaturgy section of a website must always supplement the live performance event and support issues of continuity. This includes email pushes that go out to patrons or community groups in order to drum up interest in a particular show.

More traditional channels of communication include posters, advertisements and press releases. This trio of printed information can go a long way to introducing potential spectators to images, phrases, and themes that will emerge during the live performance event. If issues of continuity are ignored, though, then this trio can do much to confuse the issue. Of course we are not suggesting that the production dramaturg write or design this material. However, a production dramaturg should have some sort of editorial input if at all possible. It is somewhat easier in an academic situation where, because funds might be less, these tasks are often taken up by already burdened faculty, staff or student volunteers who welcome the assistance. The more that the production dramaturg can spread the web of unity into this realm of the production process, the better the overall live performance event will undoubtedly be for spectators.

So You Want to be a Production Dramaturg

These sorts of publications and presentations are often what the public face of production dramaturgy becomes. As such, the production dramaturg must avoid at all costs coming off as a stuffy, professorial know-it-all. The materials generated ought to be full of high ideas presented in accessible ways to theatre patrons of all ages and levels of theatrical understanding. Herein is the complexity of developing suitable outreach and education endeavors. These challenges can sometimes be subdued if the production dramaturg has the luxury of working with creative-collaborators in an education department. They can also be tackled by conversing with other production dramaturgs about their recent ideas—both successful and not. The LMDA website provides a wonderful outlet for these types of discussions as do the listservs of organizations such as **ATHE** and **AATE**. Regardless of the communicative channel chosen, the production dramaturg must always remember that the purpose of outreach and education is to engage patrons in a variety of ways that reinforce continuity.

Chapter Glossary

AATE: American Alliance for Theatre Education is the national voice for theatre and education.

ATHE: Association for Theatre in Higher Education is an advocate for theatre and live performance within higher education organization that cultivates connections between scholarship and creative endeavors.

Educational lobby design: a design that seeks to exhibit process-based information as a way to illuminate broader processes inherent to staging the live performance

Experiential lobby design: a lobby experience that offers spectators the opportunity to engender a visceral response to the world of the play through an array of production-specific information and images, all of which is reinforced by the presence of performers in the lobby

Hard lead: Traditionally this type of first paragraph is an encapsulated version of the longer story. In general, this opening conveys the *Who, How, Where, Why, When,* and *What* of a story.

Interactive lobby design: A lobby experience offers spectators the opportunity to connect to the live performance event through an array of production-specific information and images.

Program synopsis: a recounting of the overall story of the play that does not reveal too much about major turning points while clarifying character relationships

Soft lead: Though there are several variations of this type of first paragraph, they often begin with the most interesting aspect of a story. Most importantly, this opening must convey unique ideas in an engaging way.

Chapter Seven

A Case Study of *Biloxi Blues*

By offering the creative-collaborative process used for an academic production of Neil Simon's *Biloxi Blues*, this chapter points to ways in which all of the information and exercises offered thus far might be put into action. We suggest reading closely to look for how elements overlap, converge or even diverge in synergystic ways. We have deliberately selected a university production from a moderately sized BA/MFA/PhD-granting theatre department in the US to illustrate that powerful, passionate creative-collaboration is "do-able" without extensive resources and requires only solid planning, stable persistence and substantial patience. Not only did the research by the production dramaturgs aid the director and performers but also it enriched and informed the lobby design and aspects of community outreach that always fall within the production dramaturg's purview.

Pre-Production

Choosing the Show

Biloxi Blues was selected for three primary reasons. First, the Theater Department's current talent pool included a disproportionately large number of male performers. Second, the overall season needed to include a comedy because other selections were rather dark. Third, financial exigencies of opening the season with a show that would sell tickets loomed large. The director was assigned the production and therefore faced the challenge of finding a way into the piece. Given this, the director started by looking for the inherent humanity often at the heart Neil Simon's work, which is frequently maligned as simple comedy.

Starting the Process

At the close of the spring semester ("Biloxi" would be the department's first production the following fall.), the director met a few times with production dramaturgy as well as with the set and costume designers. The production dramaturgs went about the basic "hunting and gathering" necessary to enter into conversations with their collaborators at the first full production meeting in the fall. The director was adamant that, although the United States was currently at war, the live performance event had to remain a World War II piece. Given all this, production dramaturgy refined hunting and gathering in order to arrive at the first full meeting with more period visual research relevant to these points of interest. Both the director and the set designer asked for more precise images of WWII Army life, particularly close-up views of properties like the footlocker, so the production dramaturgs focused their efforts accordingly.

By the time classes resumed, they had already provided the director and set designer with information on World War II, specifically Army barracks and the detailed photographs of footlockers, along with dramatic criticism on Neil Simon as well as his first memoir in which the period of his life that inspired "Biloxi" is covered. Over the summer break they had completed a draft of the gloss and were now working on gathering music and dance sources in anticipation of the first meeting in the fall. Contact with the director was re-established just prior to the first full meeting. This conversation established that the director wanted to foreground an overall sense of order and precision inherent to Simon's play—specifically referencing the clean, crisp lines of the barracks as illustrated by research photos from the set designer. Interestingly, the director sought to contrast this linearity with a curvaceous, feminine quality in Rowena's room, which was subsequently described by the set designer as "seductively dingy."

The First Design/Production Meeting

The contributions of production dramaturgy at the first full production team meeting included a War Department Basic Field Manual of Military Training dated 16 July 1941 as well as several WWII web sites with clear images. They also presented instructions for "The Correct Way to Make Your Bunk", "Infantry Drill Regulations", and showed the team an interactive site with detailed descriptions of each item in a footlocker and its placement. The production dramaturgs also arrived with excerpts from Neil Simon's *The Play Goes On: A Memoir*. The most notable contribution that day, however, was a query, echoed by the lighting designer, as to how the director intended to deal with "Biloxi" as a "Memory Play." With this, the meeting adjourned.

Subsequent Design Meetings

The director brought the *Declaration of Independence* to the second meeting and spoke about ways in which individuals in a group, seeking independence, leave lasting impressions of their specific personalities and contributions. The director was quite clear in the expression of a human desire "to contribute and leave a legacy" as "part of the human condition."[1] The production of this play would be no different. The director went on to correlate the diary of the character Eugene, "memoirs" as he calls it, with this notion of leaving one's mark in the world. The ideas of "leaving a mark" and "memory", the director continued, needed to carry through the entire creative-collaborative process.

The director's overarching metaphor for the production grew out of these ideas and finally centered on "getting involved in the fight", a line that was taken from Epstein at the end of Act One. "You have to get involved. You have to get in middle of it. You have to take sides. Make a contribution to the fight. Any fight…The one you believe in."[2] The director likened this fight to the production process itself, alluding to "the passion and the fire to create", to asking spectators to play an active role in their own live theatrical experience and to the director's challenge to "fight" to make this story—true with ANY story—come to life.[3] The director additionally noted Simon's use of the classic coming of age storytelling device, subsequently explicating her desire "to unfold the way in which boys discover how to discern what their beliefs are and where they fit in the grand scheme of the world." Inside the framework of WWII, the director "wanted to reveal the intimate lives of five uniquely individual young army troopers discovering their

---

1   Jennifer M. Holcombe, "Directing Biloxi Blues: Getting Involved in the Fight." (M.F.A. Thesis, Southern Illinois University Carbondale, 2008) 8.

2   Neil Simon, *Biloxi Blues* (New York: Samuel French, Inc., 1986) 48.

3   Holcombe 1-2.

identities by playing survival of the fittest in the sweltering heat of a Biloxi, Mississippi basic training camp." The director made it clear to the production dramaturgs that this production was to "carve out a small piece of history and insert this story within the greater timeline of WWII."[4]

At this second meeting in particular the production dramaturgs were asked to listen carefully, to take notes, and to reflect on what the director emphasized in making design choices so as to better pin-point how production dramaturgy could 1) generate resource materials that would best serve both the director and the live performance event and 2) assist in realizing the director's vision in practical, pragmatic ways. Needless to say, questions abounded as the meeting commenced. How might the director's ideas manifest themselves later in the lobby experience? What materials—from a vast array of WWII resources available—might be of use to the production team? Aid the rehearsal process? As the director spoke—and to the production dramaturgs' great relief—it became apparent that while insisting that the WWII setting be preserved, the director had no intention of creating a museum piece. It was obvious, as well, that the director sought to give this segment of Neil Simon's autobiographical trilogy a new reading. The director later admitted:

> I wished to take a well known play, by a well known play-wright, and revive the naked truths woven throughout what some might call a 'museum' piece of comedy. A museum piece would serve only as a re-creation or a re-mount of the original production, not one that had resonations for our current audiences. I hoped to move an audience with what might seem like a simple story, and reveal strong political and universal undertones of the play. With this production, I wanted to regain respect for Neil Simon and *Biloxi Blues*, proving that an old Simon play could still hold great theat-rical power...[5]

With the director's goals defined, the production dramaturgs began hunting and gathering and the physical task of generating the glossary

---

4   Holcombe 2.
5   Holcombe 2.

of terms and concepts while simultaneously seeking ways into the written text that would be beneficial. Their work, general before, was now focused.

Additional Meetings with the Director

In the weeks prior to auditions, the director and production dramaturgs continued to hone the production conceit. This highly collaborative time of exploration eventually culminated in a moving interpretation that focused on a number of thoughts that ultimately made their way into the rehearsal process. Particularly important to all involved was the notion of leaving one's mark. For one character in particular, that meant through song. Performers were charged with identifying how their character marked his or her place in the world. This identification added depth to character motivation, manifesting itself in active verb choices. Following the director's lead, the production dramaturgs borrowed these formative thoughts for what would later emerge as a thought-provoking lobby display.

By the third meeting, the director was deep into text preparation and cognizant of various connotations of the play's title, the geographic situation of Biloxi, Mississippi, etcetera. The director had familiarized herself with the military training manuals and drawn the conclusion that, while specific military practices might change across wars, the uniformity of the training did not. Spectators would infer the play's connection to US involvement in Iraq and Afghanistan in 2007. As the director had suspected, no updating would be required. The director recognized the playwright's interweaving of presentational moments in a largely representational play, and was ready to focus on the liminal spaces in which Eugene finds himself. With this, the production dramaturgs' work accelerated quickly.

By this point, both the sound and costume designers were well into their processes and simply touched base with the production dramaturgs if independent searches turned out to be unfruitful. The set designer had already located inspirational images in the form of WWII posters and USO "propaganda" materials. The designer sought more such images, especially depictions of the USO dance. To assist in this quest, the production dramaturgs watched films such as *Verna: USO Girl*, *Stage Door Canteen* and others from the period to see what they might find. Beyond this, the production dramaturgs continued with still image searches both online and in photography books. Of course, they continued to feed the director print matter as well, especially published letters, diaries and other firsthand accounts of WWII experiences. Ultimately, dramaturgical focus shifted toward procuring primary documents, especially three-dimensional objects for the lobby display. Attention also turned to coordinating the Pre-Show Lecture experience as well as working with Public Relations in organizing a Patrons Party that would tie into the production conceit.

Resource Materials

Creating the gloss was a straightforward process. It was surprising, however, how many topical references, literary allusions (*Anna Christie*, *Anna Karenina*, Daisy Buchanan, *Daisy Miller*, Dostoyesvky, F. Scott Fitzgerald, Kafka and more), popular culture personalities (Fred Astaire, Jack Benny, Perry Como, Joe DiMaggio, Clark Gable, etcetera), and songs ("Chattanooga Choo-Choo", "Empty Saddles in the Old Corral", "Love in Bloom") Simon included in what many mistakenly dismiss as a "simple comedy." With a young cast, the production dramaturgs took care to define products with which older performers would be familiar—like Aqua Velva. Of course, there were many military terms and place names in addition to idiosyncratic ethnic words, phrases and unflattering epithets like "kike", "Mick", and the like. The director dealt with the performers' reactions to derogatory terms related to race, ethnicity and religion, arguing that part of the play's point was the leveling process that transpires when a group of young men, many of whom had never left home before, are thrown together in basic training—a phenomena no different today. Interestingly, the production dramaturgs discovered that "Africa Hot", the excerpt from Simon's memoir read by the cast, demanded a gloss of its own as it was riddled with references to both stage and screen, included specific geographic references with regard to Simon's experience in basic training, and included racial and ethnic epithets of its own. This information was distributed and discussed during the first rehearsal.

What ultimately made this particular sequence of pre-production meetings so distinctive was that the members of the artistic team were all well-equipped to commit their own acts of dramaturgy, possessing sound and imaginative research skills and the savvy to apply their findings in relevant ways. In addition, the director was particularly adept at picking and choosing ways in which the production dramaturgs' talents were to be deployed in maintaining continuity.

Resource Pack Table of Contents for *Biloxi Blues*
Southern Illinois University Carbondale
Jordan Vakselis, Production Dramaturg (Anne Fletcher, Advisor)
Jennifer M. Holcombe, Director

Table of Contents
Biloxi Blues Production History
Neil Simon: List of Plays and Biography
Summary of the "Eugene Trilogy" (*Brighton Beach Memoirs*,
Biloxi Blues and *Broadway Bound*)
Excerpts from Neil Simon's Memoirs: *The Play Goes On*
"Africa Hot" Glossary
WWII Timelines and Maps
USO Images ("Propaganda")
Army Ranks
Basic Training
Eisenhower Note and Background

Rehearsals

By the first rehearsal, the director had found a retired Army trainer to work with the cast. The arc of the rehearsal process was clearly mapped for all involved. Specific to the performers, the process would begin with ensemble-building, a journaling exercise that emulated Eugene's writings as well as other experiential/improvisational exercises meant to set the world of the play on the bodies of the performers. With this foundation, the director would proceed to traditional blocking and timing rehearsals. Because such a solid foundation was set during pre-production meetings, production dramaturgy during the rehearsal period focused largely on unifying outreach and patron services endeavors with the overall production conceit. Consistent communication between the director and production dramaturgs was maintained through both stage management and weekly production meetings.

Well in advance of production week, the dramaturgy team discovered that PBS would air Ken Burns' WWII documentary *The War* during the production week of *Biloxi Blues*. In addition, the local affiliate station WSIU was seeking interviewers for a national oral history project documenting the memories of WWII veterans. The documentary, of course, complimented the director's notions of "marking" and chronicled memories. The production dramaturgs quickly established a relationship with a public information representative at WSIU hoping both to generate mutually beneficial outreach opportunities and to extend a dialogue beyond the live performance event of *Biloxi Blues*.

Meanwhile, the director formulated a series of questions that the lobby experience needed to address. These were similar to the questions posed to cast members during the first rehearsal: "How do we document our history?"; "What does independence mean to you?" and "How can we bridge the gap between 1943 and 2007?" Since the director determined early in the process that the idea of leaving one's mark would concretely manifest itself during the rehearsal process in efficacious ways, the performers wrote personal memoirs and the rehearsal process was visually documented through still photographs and film. These varied documents eventually became the closing section of the lobby design.

Production and Beyond

The Lobby Design

The lobby design systematically addressed each of the questions posed by the director. In doing so, the production dramaturgs blended elements of both an educational and interactive design. They started this process by gathering period artifacts through contacts with faculty, family and friends. This tactic led to the procurement of dog tags, written correspondence, a WWII photo album, and even authentic uniforms. Because of the publicity generated by the production's affiliation with the television station, a local resident even offered his framed newspapers from the day after D-Day. Dress forms were obtained for the uniforms and a color scheme inspired by khaki and camouflage was adopted.

Img. 7.1 *Biloxi Blues* Glass Case with journals. McLeod Theatre. Dir.: Jennifer Holcombe. Photo: Robert Holcombe.

Early brainstorming sessions the director held with performers on ways in which individuals leave their mark on society and in the world resulted in a list of documentation styles that included letters, journals, memoirs, films and videos, photographs, scrapbooks, recorded telephone calls, storytelling and/or plays, markings (carvings, graffiti, etcetera), music, and declarations/bills/government documents. Each of these manifested themselves within the display, which was sited in accordance with the director's vision of how the spectators needed to enter the world of the play. Spectators were first introduced to historical artifacts, including the period uniforms, before they proceeded down the long narrow lobby to a section dedicated to the production process. This educational component included a streaming video of the rehearsal process, still photographs, the performers' journals, designers' renderings and inspirational images. 1940s tunes were piped into the space as well. Lastly, spectators arrived at a US flag and a framed replica of the *Declaration of Independence*.

The director had visited the WWII Museum in New Orleans and was particularly drawn to a display there that visually emphasized how

Japan and Germany's troops far outnumbered those of the US 4:1 at the outset of WWII. She wanted a similar visual comparison between the numbers of US troops deployed in September 2007 versus September 1943 through the creation of parallel lists. Unfortunately, the production dramaturgs could not find a way to effectively execute this plan and turned instead to a vintage "Uncle Sam Wants You" poster accompanied by a WWII scarf and flight helmet, juxtaposing them with 2007 Army recruitment material in order to construct the "Then" and "Now" section.

The Pre-Show Lecture

Collaboration with the local television station continued, and posters advertising *The War* as well as flyers with a schedule of when the program would air were included in the display. The station sought volunteers to interview WWII veterans, so it seemed a logical choice to have the station representative give the Pre-Show lecture (and at the same time "plug" for volunteers). The Pre-Show lecture included a brief excerpt of the program, an explanation of the Library of Congress's Veterans History Project and a plea for volunteers and/or recommendations of local veterans to call on to share their stories.

Audience Development and Community Outreach

Finding the Veterans

The Theater Department was certain that *Biloxi Blues* held appeal for veterans of all conflicts, particularly those of WWII. As a producing organization, though, its databases of potential spectators from this population were limited at best and proved much more of a challenge for Public Relations/Marketing than the usual production marketing. Again, the alliance production dramaturgy established with WSIU became crucial as the station willingly shared its lists of local veterans and joined forces with the department in promoting both the Ken Burns documentary and the production of Simon's play. A screening of *The War* was already scheduled at a restored movie theatre in a neighboring community. As part of this partnership, the director and cast members attended the screening in costume with flyers to advertise the production.

Img. 7.2 *Biloxi Blues* USO Dance Patron Party-Serving Punch. Southern Illinois University Carbondale. Dir.: Jennifer Holcombe. Photo: Robert Holcombe.

The Patron's Party

As a result of the association with WSIU, the opening of *Biloxi Blues* warranted a special social event for its patrons (donors). The director and production dramaturgs desired a social gathering that was more visibly connected with the play's subject matter and/or style of production than the usual patron events. Over the course of pre-production meetings, the production team had become particularly enamored with the USO Dance scene, and it was natural to draw on it for the party. It took some persuasion on the parts of the director and production dramaturgs, however, to convince those in marketing that this was a viable idea. After some heavy persuasion, which was aided by the production dramaturgs' offer to take over the planning of the event, the Marketing Director was "won over" and both enthusiasm and involvement swelled. A huge USO banner was hung in the laboratory theater where the event was held. Finger sandwiches and punch highlighted the menu. With the help of the resident Costume Designer and

Costume Shop Manager, female student and faculty volunteers dressed in period attire, creating the illusion of the "stars" who volunteered to serve the troops at WWII USO halls. The sound designer provided period music, and one couple, including the actress playing Daisy, took the floor first with period dance moves as a way to encourage patron participation. The guest list included not only the department's patrons but also members of the local Veterans Association chapter along with the representative from WSIU.

Outreach events such as the *Biloxi Blues* USO Dance Patron Party are sometimes as meaningful for the organizers and participants as they are for the targeted community that does not witness behind-the-scenes activities. A tired faculty member, for example, entered the dressing room thinking, "I can't believe I said I would dress up like this and serve punch!" to be met by excited undergraduates, already dressed, one of whom exclaimed, "I can't believe we're having a USO Dance! I called my mother." Others were touched by the grace with which the young sound designer and "Daisy" took the floor for the first dance and the manner in which a lovely undergraduate, in 1940s garb, left the punch table to invite a WWII veteran to dance. These sorts of para-theatrical moments may not seem to amount to much in terms of ticket sales, but they may reap rewards later in terms of good-will and community outreach. The production dramaturg involved in these types of outreach efforts must remember that someone who has a genuinely personalized experience in the theatre will likely return sooner rather than later.

In the Classroom

Outreach and education extends not only beyond the walls of the Theatre Department or professional theatre venue but also to its own constituencies—in the case of academic theatre, the student popu-lation. At Southern Illinois University Carbondale, "teaching to the season" is a methodology employed in at least three distinct classroom settings—THEA 101 (an introductory course for non-majors), THEA 220 (the equivalent beginning class for Theater majors), and THEA 354 (Theatre History and Literature I and II). Syllabi for these courses are designed thematically rather than adhering to strict chronology and alter each semester according to the production calendar. Principle concepts and subject matter remain constant, but examples are drawn from departmental productions that students read as well as view.

Students in THEA 101 purchase a Course Packet to which the production dramaturgs contribute in advance of the semester. Assignments are crafted around the live performance event to reinforce concepts covered in class such as presentational and representational theatre. In this case, production dramaturgy encouraged special attention to the memory play aspects of the text in addition to elements of comedy. Experiential exercises were devised, in this instance paralleling the director's notions of how people leave their mark, and student Performance Response Essay prompts began with a paragraph addressing reactions to the lobby display. Students also viewed excerpts from the film version of the play and were asked to compare specific moments or elements to what they saw on stage. In the Theatre History and Literature course, students were asked to contemplate how different playwrights, across time and place, address particular thematic concerns. For example, having read *Lysistrata* earlier in the semester these students were not only able to apply elements of comedy and presentational staging techniques to their pre-show study of *Biloxi Blues*, but also to the post-show written material about how war was dealt with and how issues of ethnicity were depicted in each play. These explorations of Simon's play proved to be even more effective in the classroom than either instructors or students had anticipated.

Post-Production: The Veterans Hospital

In exchange for WSIU's assistance in publicizing *Biloxi Blues*, the production dramaturgs had promised the station representative that at least they (and possibly a few others) would conduct interviews with WWII veterans as part of the station's contribution to a nationwide oral history project (to be housed at the Library of Congress). All in all, about half a dozen participants attended a training session and prepared to conduct the interviews. All of the veterans to be interviewed were patients at a local VA hospital. Armed with a digital recorder, a little nervous about this foray into the realm of oral history, and with a review of the particulars provided on each veteran, the interviewers proceeded. The resulting interviews varied in quality and length, through no fault of the interviewers, but due to circumstances beyond their control such as the gravity of the veteran's illness. One bed-ridden veteran on oxygen who had told his story in history classrooms in better days spoke softly but with determination for well over one hour. As with the Patron Party planning and execution, participation in this activity was limited, but again, the goodwill engendered and the collaboration with the local television station will not be forgotten by those involved. These are acts of dramaturgy that, like Eugene's memoirs, will leave an indelible mark on the world far beyond the live performance event.

Chapter Eight

Closing Thoughts for Instructors and Student Dramaturgs

We began *The Process of Dramaturgy* with a comment regarding how acts of dramaturgy are committed whenever a written text makes its way from the page to the stage. Given this, we set about illustrating ways that these acts could be accomplished. While we opened by arguing that it was not our intention to provide a definition of production dramaturgy or the production dramaturg's role, by the nature of crafting this handbook we have, to some extent, unintentionally done just that. To this end, then, we hope that this handbook has provided helpful suggestions.

While we have been fortunate enough to be in places that have afforded us multiple opportunities to practice creative-collaboration as production dramaturgs, we acknowledge that not all theatre departments offer dramaturgy courses or have the personnel to assign a production dramaturg for every production in the season of plays. In reality, some of our own professional aspirations have met with resistance as companies "tighten the purse strings", arguing they can not afford to designate someone solely to this "expendable" area of creative-collaboration. In these instances, no doubt, someone—be it director, design team member, or intern—completed the tasks of the production dramaturg, sharing information unearthed in the process. We maintain, however, that it is the depth to which a dedicated production dramaturg engages in the processes outlined that sets them apart from other members of the artistic team. Nevertheless, it is to those who "commit acts of dramaturgy" that we have directed *The Process of Dramaturgy* as a way not only to open a dialogue among practitioners regarding the integration of dramaturgical processes into their own praxis, but also as to how producing organizations will integrate production dramaturgy into their overall preparation.

So You Want to be a Production Dramatrug?

Throughout *The Process of Dramaturgy* we have implicitly directed many of our comments to aspiring and nascent production dramaturgs—those who seek a career in this specific aspect of production, be it in academic theatre or at a professional venue. Suitably, then, we close with some suggestions on where to go from here.

An Exercise on Immediacy

What Can I Do Right Now?

Volunteer! Volunteer! Volunteer!

Instructions

1. Familiarize yourself with the department or theatre's programming.

2. Determine in what area(s) you are willing to volunteer.

3. Figure out, in advance, how many hours per week you can offer to work.

Seldom will either an academic theatre program or a professional company refuse to take on a volunteer.

An Exercise on "The Ranks"

Who Commits Acts of Dramaturgy in the Professional World?

It is interesting as well as practical to become familiar with "who does what" and "who reports to whom" in the professional theatre before heading out into that world. As we mentioned much earlier, dramaturgical tasks are often dispersed throughout several offices. Though the content of web sites change, "job titles" often remain the same.

Instructions

1. Go to the websites of a few well-known theatre companies in your region and see if their organizational chart is available for viewing. If not, then see if there is a listing of the company's complete staff.

2. In either case, note whether a production dramaturg is listed. A literary manager? A person for Education or Community Outreach?

3. Review the theatre's programming. Are there special events such as panels or symposia? Are Resource Packets available on line?

4. Many organizational charts list the production dramaturg on a par with the director. Locate a position on the organizational chart or personnel list that obviously involves dramaturgical tasks and then review the positions directly below it. (Note: Generic organizational charts are available in books on arts management.)

This type of "hunting and gathering" is an important tool for both the up-and-coming and practiced production dramaturg as it provides a wider view of how acts of dramaturgy are committed and by whom within the broader theatre community.

An Exercise on Education

Finding Graduate Programs in Dramaturgy

For those interested in committing acts of dramaturgy as a profession, further training is needed to hone skills, gifts and talents.

Instructions

1. Consult the LMDA listserv for current discussions regarding current graduate opportunities

2. Consult a reputable guide to graduate schools (such as Peterson's), hard copy or online (Look at programs in Dramatic Literature, Theatre History, Performance Studies, etcetera as well as Dramaturgy.)

3. Generate a top five list and visit each school.

4. Consider what the alumni from these programs are doing now.

5. Consider who is on faculty and what are they doing professionally.

6. Find out what kind of financial support programs will offer.

7. Inquire if getting teaching experience is part of the process.

8. See if there are opportunities to work on campus productions.

Perhaps a few have come to this handbook from disciplines outside of theatre, previously having only a tangential interest in live performance and a curiosity regarding production dramaturgy in particular. For these individuals we suggest considering a more general program of graduate study in theatre, an M.A., perhaps, before heading into a terminal degree track.

An Exercise on Employment

Finding an Internship, Apprenticeship or Paid Position

Familiarize yourself with job postings such as those on *ArtSearch*, available through the Theatre Communications Group (www.tcg.org). Read these in tandem with the organizational charts and/or personnel listings derived from the earlier exercise.

Instructions

1. Locate and study particular theatre companies that serve your region. Many professional theatre web sites list and describe areas for which they take interns or apprentices.

2. Do not become discouraged if production dramaturgy, per se, is not listed.

3. Look at Education/Outreach, or Literary Management, and write the company to inquire as to what they offer and expect.

Some may find that an internship or apprenticeship is an excellent way to prepare for graduate study. Once in the professional theatre world, though, a small number of individuals may discover that working their way "up through the ranks" is the best path because there may be aspects of work in the professional theatre that are more appealing than graduate study or teaching. A few might decide to apply to graduate school right after completing an undergraduate degree, move on to work in the field and then return for a terminal degree. Those actively engaged as actors or directors, designers, writers, critics, or theatre history/dramatic literature instructors may use a combination of these suggestions as a way to "re-tool" a bit in order to remain abreast of dialogue in the discipline.

Interestingly, each of us came to production dramaturgy through various routes, and we have found that no one career trajectory is better than another—so make sure to take note of how daily lived experiences relate to acts of dramaturgy in noteworthy ways.

Appendix A

Theatrical -isms

Essential Elements of 20th century Artistic Movements

NATURALISM

Slice of Life	• No plot as such—simply everything that happened • All settings, costumes, dialog, etc. must be complete and exactly as in real life—the real thing on stage
Focus	Society and its problems as reflected in people placed in specific situations
Goal	Objectively (scientifically) observe a situation and find a solution (Cultural Darwinism)
Theorists	Comte and Darwin
Artists	Zola and Hauptmann

REALISM

Objective View	• Carefully constructed plot—cause to effect with exposition in motivated conversation • All settings, costumes, dialog, business, etc. must reflect and reveal character—carefully chosen and described by the author
Focus	Individuals and their psychological motivations
Goal	Understand people and predict behavior--if an individual life is improved perhaps society will gradually change
Theorist	Darwin
Artists	Ibsen, Chekhov, Shaw

SYMBOLISM

Subjective	• Play is not a story—episodic, disjointed, and distorted • Word is dominant- poetic and allusive • Dialog chanted intoned or sung • Gesture stylized • Spectacle is essential and atmospheric only—mood <u>not</u> place important • Objects as symbols of the internal state of the characters • Actors and settings generalized, depersonalized signs
Focus	<u>The spiritual </u>(not religious) side of life reflected in the unconscious mind
Goal	• Reject logical, reasoned scientific behavior and suggest the mystery of the universe and celebrate it • Drama a sacred and mysterious rite and a means of cognition
Theorists	Freud and Einstein
Artists	Maeterlink and Claudel (Poe and Wagner)

SURREALISM

Subjective /Objective juxtaposed	• Metaphoric plot—based on automatic writing—unrelated scenes juxtaposed—everyday made mythical and the mythical made familiar • Juxtaposition of the familiar and the unfamiliar dominate all elements of spectacle—distortion and realism mixed to create a sense of super-realism—a dream state • Spontaneity and strong imagery the key
Focus	<u>Unconscious mind as the site of understanding the world</u>. The purpose is to free the unconscious mind
Goal	Understand and access the <u>real</u> process of thought and transform the world through associational patterns that lead to new perceptions
Theorist	Freud
Artists	Breton and Cocteau (Artaud in his writings)

EXPRESSIONISM

Subjective	• Eyes of the central character (Dream Plays) (looking inward)Word is dominant- poetic and allusive • Fragmentary plot--audience must provide connections between disparate elements—multiple focus—unity of motif or theme • Search or pilgrimage common • Central character often Christ-like and sacrificed • Action seen only through the eyes of the central character—all other characters are generic • Dialog is telegraphic • Settings, costumes, sound and lighting are distorted and sharp contrasts appear everywhere as elements of spectacle
Focus	Reformation of society through the human spirit
Goal	• Truth exists only within humanity—external reality should be reshaped to match the internal reality and allow the human spirit to reach higher • Allegory as Nightmare
Theorists	Freud and Jung
Artists	Strindberg and O'Neill (Van Gogh and Gauguin)

— Courtesy of Sarah J. Blackstone

Appendix B

Sample Syllabus

This is the skeleton for a semester-long overview of production dramaturgy that culminates in generating a production book for a live performance event to be staged in the near future.

Required Assignments

Classic Play and "New Ways"

After reading and discussing the chosen classic play and Mark Fortier's *theatre/theory: an introduction.* 2nd Edition (London: Routledge, 2003) each learner will complete a 900-1200 word essay that "reads" the play through a particular theoretical lens in order to arrive at a "New Way" of producing this classic text.

Outreach

After reading and discussing the assigned play, each learner will be responsible for generating age-and audience-appropriate outreach materials as if the School of Theatre were producing the play next season.

Musical/Antecedent

Having read a Broadway musical and the source from which it came, each learner will generate a handout and oral presentation outlining exactly to what extent the play was translated, abbreviated, violated, etcetera in its conversion to a musical.

New Play Respondent

You are required to attend a reading of a new play and to participate in the post-reading talkback.

Production Project/Casebook

This project asks each learner to prepare a pre-production resource book for the director of one of the shows in the season of plays following procedures and suggestions given by Irelan, Fletcher and Dubiner in Chapter One of this book.

Exploration 1: What is Dramaturgy?

Day 1: Overview of Course; Outline tasks; Discuss Glossary and other background information.

Day 2: Read and Discuss a variety of perspectives on Dramaturgical Sensibilities.

Discuss and devise a working definition to be used for the term "dramaturg."

Day 3: Starting Where You Are

Self-assessment and Reflection on present skills and the applicability to committing acts of dramaturgy

Exploration 2: Preliminary Steps

Day 4: The Dramaturg's Production Book

Discuss structure and content.

Assign a play and divide tasks among learners.

Day 5: Making Contact and Letter(s) of Agreement

Day 6: Generating Outreach Ideas and Developing Talking Points

Day 7: Pre-Production Material on chosen play due

Exploration 3: Developing New Works and the "New Poetics"

Day 8: Revisit Form(s) and Style(s)

Review Genre

Discuss Aristotle's Six Elements of Drama

Day 9: The Writer's Friend; or. How to Listen, Learn and Ask Questions

Read a new text and draft some questions.

Day 10: Discuss and Practice the Post-Show Discussion

Day 11: Read Paul Castagno, *New Playwriting Strategies: A Language-Based Approach to Playwriting* (London: Routledge, 2001) Preface, 1, 2, and 3.

Day 12: Read Castagno 4, 5, 6

Day 13: Read Castagno 7, 8, 9

Day 14: Read Castagno 10 and 11

Day 15:   Discuss and Dissect a Language-Based play using Castagno's model

Exploration 4: The Musical and Antecedent; or, Literary Translation

Day 16:   Brief History of the US Musical
          Come with Musical/Antecedent chosen

Day 17:   Read and Discuss *Romeo and Juliet* and Elizabethan Drama

Day 18:   Read, discuss and compare *Romeo and Juliet* and *West Side Story*

Day 19:   Musical/Antecedent work day

Day 20:   Present Musical/Antecedent findings

Day 21:   Present Musical/Antecedent findings

Exploration 5: Critical Theory

Day 22:   Read and discuss Fortier 1-81.
          Assign Classic Play and "New Way"

Day 23:   Read and discuss Fortier 82-150

Day 24:   Read and discuss Fortier 151-222

Day 25:   Classic Play and "New Way" assignment work day

Day 26:   Present findings

Day 27:   Present findings

Exploration 6: Outreach

Day 28:   Return to Ideas from Day 6 and expand
          Assign Outreach exercises

Day 29:   Lobby Displays, Program Notes, Newsletter Articles, and other materials

Day 30:   Lesson Plans and Resource Materials

Day 31:   Report on Outreach exercises

FINAL: Production Book for Season of Plays due

Appendix C

A Resource List

Play Texts

Jess Borgeson, Adam Long and Daniel Singer, *The Complete Works of William Shakespeare (abridged)* (NY: Applause Books, 1994). Print.

Charles Dickens, *A Christmas Carol* (London: Charles Dickens, 1843). Print. Adapted by Scott R. Irelan and James Russell Couch (1999) and Barbara Field (1978).

Brian Friel, *Dancing at Lughnasa* (NY: Dramatists Play Service Inc., 1992). Print.

Lorraine Hansberry, *A Raisin in the Sun* (NY: Random House, 1958). Print.

Joan Holden, *Nickel and Dimed* (NY: Dramatist's Play Service, 2005). Print.

Alan Jay Lerner with music by Frederick Loewe, *My Fair Lady* (NY: Signet Classics, 2006). Print.

Steve Martin, *The Underpants* (NY: Hyperion Books, 2002). Print.

Arthur Miller, *The Crucible* (NY: Dramatists Play Service Inc., 1953). Print.

Eric Overmyer, *On the Verge* (NY: Broadway Play Publishing Inc, 1988). Print.

William Shakespeare, *The Taming of the Shrew*. Ed. Brian Morris. (London: The Arden Shakespeare, 1981). Print. Adapted by Scott R. Irelan, Catherine Weidner and Krista Scott (2008).

--- *The Tempest*. Ed. Virginia Mason Vaughan and Alden T. Vaughan. (London: The Arden Shakespeare, 1999). Print. Adapted by Julie Felise Dubiner and Marc Masterson (2008).

--- *Titus Andronicus*. Ed. Jonathan Bate. (London: The Arden Shakespeare, 2003). Print. Adapted by Scott R. Irelan, Catherine Weidner and Krista Scott (2008).

--- *King Richard III*. Ed. Antony Hammond. (London: The Arden Shakespeare, 1981). Print. Adapted by Kristin Horton and Scott R. Irelan (2009).

Neil Simon, *Biloxi Blues* (NY: Samuel French, 1986). Print.

Wole Soyinka, *Death and the King's Horseman* (NY: WW Norton & Co, Inc., 2002). Print.

Thornton Wilder, *Our Town: A Play in Three Acts* (NY: Samuel French, Inc., 1938). Print.

Books

Bert Cardullo, *What is Dramaturgy?* (New York: Peter Lang, 1995). Print.

Paul Castagno, *New Playwriting Strategies: A Language-Based Approach to Playwriting* (London: Routledge, 2001). Print.

Critical Theory and Performance: Revised and Enlarged Edition. Ed. Joseph Roach and Janelle G. Reinelt. (Ann Arbor: Michigan UP, 2007). Print.

Dramaturgy in American Theater: A Sourcebook. Ed. Susan Jonas et al. (New York: Harcourt Brace College Publishers, 1997). Print.

Mark Fortier, *theatre/theory: an introduction*. 2nd Edition (London: Routledge, 2003). Print.

Andrew James Hartley, *The Shakespearean Dramaturg: A Theoretical and Practical Guide* (NY: Palgrave Macmillan, 2005). Print.

Mary Luckhurst, *Dramaturgy: A Revolution in Theatre* (Cambridge: Cambridge UP, 2008). Print.

Geoffrey S. Proehl, *Toward a Dramaturgical Sensibility: Landscape and Journey* (Madison: Fairleigh Dickinson UP, 2008). Print.

Judith Rudakoff and Lynn M. Thompson, *Between the Lines: The Process of Dramaturgy* (Toronto: Playwrights Canada Press, 2002). Print.

Cathy Turner and Synne Behrndt, *Dramaturgy and Performance* (NY: Palgrave Macmillan, 2008). Print.

Periodicals

Text and Performance Quarterly (London: Routledge). Print.

Theatre Research International (Cambridge: Cambridge Journals). Print. Web.

Theatre Topics (Maryland: Johns Hopkins UP). Print. Web.

Web-based Periodical Databases

JSTOR: The Scholarly Journal Archive. The Andrew W. Mellon Foundation. Web. 8 September 2009.

Project MUSE: Scholarly Journals Online. The Johns Hopkins University Press in collaboration with The Milton S. Eisenhower Library. Web. 8 September 2009.

Websites

Actor's Equity Association. www.actorsequity.org. Web. 8 September 2009.

The International Alliance of Stage Employees, Moving Picture Technicians, Artists and Allied Crafts of the United States, Its Territories and Canada, AFL-CIO, CLC. www.iatse-intl.org/home.html. Web. 8 September 2009.

Literary Managers and Dramaturgs of the Americas. www.lmda.org. Web. 8 September 2009.

Chapter One Sources

Glossary

Oxford English Dictionary (Oxford: Oxford Press, 2007). Print. Web.

<www.thesaurus.com>, Lexico Publishing Group, 2008. Web.

<www.dictionary.com>, Lexico Publishing Group, 2008. Web.

Susan Mayhew, *A Dictionary of Geography* (Oxford: Oxford UP, 2004) Web.

James Trager, *People's Chronology* (New York: Holt, 1992). Print.

Plays, Playwrights, and Production History

Internet Broadway Data Base www.ibdb.com. Web.

Internet Off-Broadway Database www.iobdb.com. Web.

The New York Times Index. (New York: *New York Times*, 1913-). Print. Web.

The Columbia Encyclopedia of Modern Drama. Eds. Evert Sprinchorn and Gabrielle Cody. (New York: Columbia UP, 2007). Print.

The World Encyclopedia of Contemporary Theatre, Vol. 1-6. Ed Don Rubin. (London: Routledge, 1994-2000). Print.

Black Literature Criticism: Excerpts from Criticism of the Most Significant Works of Black Authors over the past 200 years. Ed. James Draper. (Detroit: Gale Research, 1992). Print.

Twentieth-Century Literary Criticism [148+ vols.] (Detroit: Gale Research, 1978-). Print.

Socio-cultural Information

The New Grove Dictionary of Music and Musicians (29 vols.). Ed. Stanley Sadie. (New York: Grove, 2001). Print.

St. James Encyclopedia of Popular Culture (5 vols). Eds. Tom and Sara Pendergast. (Detroit: St. James, 2000). Print.

Encyclopedia of African-American Culture and History: The Black Experience in the Americas (5 vols.). Ed. Colin A. Palmer. (Detroit: MacMillan Reference, 2006). Print.

The Humanistic Tradition, Fourth Edition (2 Vols.). Ed. Gale K. Fiero. (Boston: McGraw-Hill, 2002). Print.

Encyclopedia of Politics and Religion. Ed. Robert Wuthnow. (Washington DC: CQ Press, 2007). Print.

Timetables of History. Eds. Bernard Grun and Eva Simpson. (Simon and Schuster, 2005). Print.

Other Valuable Sources

Production Casebooks and Monographs on Plays or Playwrights

Project MUSE: Scholarly Journals Online. The Johns Hopkins University Press in collaboration with The Milton S. Eisenhower Library, 2008. Web.

JSTOR: The Scholarly Journal Archive. The Andrew W. Mellon Foundation, 2008. Web.

<www.questia.com>. Questia Media America, 2008. Web.

Cambridge Companion to _____ or *Cambridge History of* _____ publications

*Oxford Companion to*_____ publications